CLOWNING IN ROME

also by HENRI J. M. NOUWEN

Aging

Compassion

Creative Ministry

The Genesee Diary

The Inner Voice of Love

Lifesigns

Reaching Out

The Return of the Prodigal Son

The Road to Daybreak

Seeds of Hope: A Henri Nouwen Reader
(Bob Durback, Ed.)

The Wounded Healer

Henri J. M. Nouwen

FOREWORD BY SUE MOSTELLER, C.S.J.

DOUBLEDAY

NEW YORK LONDON TORONTO SYDNEY AUCKLAND

CLOWNING IN ROME

REFLECTIONS ON SOLITUDE,
CELIBACY, PRAYER, AND
CONTEMPLATION

IMAGE BOOKS

AN IMAGE BOOK

PUBLISHED BY DOUBLEDAY

a division of Random House, Inc.

1540 Broadway, New York, New York 10036

IMAGE, DOUBLEDAY, and the portrayal of a deer drinking from a stream are
trademarks of Doubleday, a division of Random House, Inc.

First Image Books edition published 1979.

"Solitude and Community" first appeared in the No. 48, 1978 issue of *UISG Bulletin*,
Copyright © 1978 by International Union of Superiors General.

"Celibacy and the Holy" first appeared under the title "Celibacy" in the Winter 1978,
Vol. 27, No.2 issue of *Pastoral Psychology*, Copyright © 1978 by Human Sciences Press.

"Prayer and Thought" first appeared under the title "Unceasing Prayer" in the July
29–August 5, 1978, issue of *America*, Copyright © 1978 by America Press.

"Contemplation and Caring" first appeared under the title "Contemplation and
Ministry" in the June 1978 issue of *Sojourners*, Copyright © 1978
by People's Christian Coalition.

Book design by Fearn Cutler de Vicq de Cumptich

Library of Congress Cataloging-in-Publication Data

Nouwen, Henri J. M.
Clowning in Rome.
1. Spiritual life—Catholic authors—Addresses, essays, lectures. 2. Monastic
and religious life—Addresses, essays, lectures. I. Title.
BX2350.2.N67   248'.89

Library of Congress Catalog Card Number 78-22423

ISBN 0-385-49999-X

In memory of a very humble man

POPE PAUL VI

ACKNOWLEDGMENTS

 his book has its origin in four lectures given to the English-speaking community in Rome.

First of all, I want to thank Harold Darcy for inviting me to spend a semester at the North American College in Rome and for offering me the opportunity to present the lectures on celibacy and contemplation. I am also grateful to Peter Slocombe for asking me to share some reflections on prayer with the students of the Beda College and to

Josephine Rucker for convincing me to speak about solitude to the members of the Unione Internazionale Superiore Generali.

I owe a special word of appreciation to Enrico Garzilli and Matthew Clark for their supportive criticisms, to Stephen Leahy and Phil Zaeder for their stylistic corrections, and to Ida Bertoni, Paul Holmes, and David Lancaster for their secretarial assistance.

I want also to express my sincere thanks to Fred Hofheinz and the staff of the Lilly Endowment for creating the possibility of spending time away from "home."

A final word of thanks goes to my friend John Mogabgab, who—as in my other writing—has given his invaluable assistance and support.

CONTENTS

FOREWORD TO THE REVISED EDITION OF *CLOWNING IN ROME*

As a child, Henri was fascinated by the circus and the fascination never left him. For many years and especially during the last year of his life, he was preparing to write a novel based on the circus related to the spiritual life. It was never written because of his untimely death.

On a visit to Rome in the late seventies, Henri gradually identifies the "clowns of Rome" as those who are wasting their time with the little, broken, unattractive, sometimes violent people who suffer and for whom no one else seems to care. Observing the lives of these unusual clowns pouring out their life energies to care for brothers and sisters in a city of pilgrims and violence, Henri is inspired to speak of the clownlike foolishness of choosing to live a life of love and service for God and others.

In the first chapters, "Solitude and Community," Henri describes this chosen life of love and service as one that is "alone but not lonely." He teaches us that choosing to be alone in solitude nurtures the tenderness, peacefulness, and inner freedom to move closer to one another or, if necessary, to withdraw from one another. Solitude, he says, is the gentle guide to all forms of intimacy. In solitude our deep longings to be loved unconditionally, and to love with our whole beings are uncovered, and in solitude we more readily meet the One who calls us Beloved. Being alone indirectly transforms relationships and builds community. Community, according to Henri, is not a group of individuals huddling together out of fear or driven together by common anger, but community is a Body of people, bound by a common heritage—all children of a personal God.

Another facet of this life of love and service is about "sacred space." Henri calls it "Celibacy and the Holy." He gets to his subject by first describing the churches of Rome, the beautiful framed empty spaces, the not useful, not practical, tranquil spaces that are empty most of the time but are set aside for the Holy and are always "sacred." These framed empty spaces are an image, he says, to give meaning to celibacy in our contemporary society. Aware of our human condition of aloneness as never before, Henri points out how we are led to believe that relationships— and especially relationships of intimacy—will free us from our deepest pain. What follows is disillusionment, anguish, resentment, bitterness, violence, and rage. At the heart of all intimacy though there can be a holy vacancy, a space reserved for the author of Love. This is a deeply personal space, which, protected and nurtured, is also fertile ground for mature love and friendship. A few people may witness more radically to holy emptiness by not marrying and by dedicating themselves to a consecrated life of vowed celibacy. By not marrying and by abstaining from the most intimate expression of human love, the celibate, like the clown, chooses foolishness, but always with the hope that the God of Love, who fills the empty, sacred space, will be enough. In Henri's vision though, the practice of celibacy is for each person, partnered or single. It is a gift, to be received from the One who dwells within us and who makes our inner sanctum, sacred.

"Communing with Love" is another element in the life of love and service. Henri names it "Prayer and Thought." A true teacher, Henri explains with imagery and passion the transformative possibilities where unceasing thinking becomes continual conversation with Love. He is convinced that prayer is the channeling of our helter-skelter thought patterns out of fearful isolation into fearless conversation with the One who loves us unconditionally. Henri is respectful of the time it takes to give our thoughts over to transformation. Time is needed, he says, to overcome our deep fears, stinginess, and resistance, and to willingly turn all our aspirations, all our thinking, all our lives, into a dialogue of love. "Discipline," an unpopular word, describes the path of the disciple, who follows and who practices generous and unambiguous acts of love according to one's particular life, work, heritage, and personality. Choosing supportive disciplines leads us to greater and greater possibilities for real intimacy in our encounter with Love Itself.

The final practice for those on the spiritual journey is "loving and caring," which Henri entitles "Contemplation and Caring." Michelangelo, contemplating a block of white marble, envisaged a loving mother holding her dead son on her lap. A skilled sculptor, Michelangelo "uncovered" what he saw in the marble. Like the great artist, Henri uncovers for us a life of contemplation and caring moving us from opaqueness to transparency in three of our central relationships; with nature, with time, and with each other. Pollution on the rise is a sign of the gap separating us from receiving and cultivating the gift of nature with gratitude, admiration, and profound awe. Time, too, seems to threaten and enslave us, and is no longer a friendly opportunity, a seed, carrying within itself new possibilities for growth, new life, and love. And finally, our history of painful, broken relationships with parents, partners, brothers, sisters, and friends prevents us from receiving and giving from our precious and true belonging to one another as children of God. To contemplate the beauty and mystery of our God is deeply healing, and gives profound significance to our relationships with the universe, with time, and with one another. Contemplation is, according to Henri, a special "window" in the spiritual life that allows us to view our world as one that points beyond itself. Caring and taking responsibility for one another follows this recognition of the unique and mysterious value of our lives.

As I revised this book for publication, I was amazed at the wisdom and relevancy of this small text. Henri would have been in his forties when he wrote these lines, but they reveal timeless and universal insight into the foolishness and the wisdom of choosing to follow a spiritual path. For this Revised Edition, I took the liberty to change much of the language that seemed old and somewhat yellow around the edges. Knowing Henri as I did, I presumed that, had he been revising it, he would have done likewise in order to reach out to a more universal audience.

Our cultures have pretty much put aside the values of solitude, celibacy, prayer, and contemplation. As a result, we experience emptiness in our hearts and our relationships. *Clowning in Rome* will perhaps inspire us to risk to be touched by those in our homes and on our streets that we would rather put aside and forget. The homeless, belligerent, rejected, violent, lost, uncooperative, and vulnerable people are the prophets of today beckoning us to become clowns in the circus of life, where we foolishly squander our enormous energies of love and generosity. Henri is convincing about this being the way to experience the foolishness and the joy of being beloved children of God, and of loving others with faithfulness, energy, and hope.

—Sue Mosteller, C.S.J.
Henri Nouwen Literary Centre
January 2000

INTRODUCTION

On the periphery of the circus

This small book was born in Rome. I had always wondered what it would be like to live in Rome for more than a
few weeks of vacation. When the staff of the North American College invited me to join them for five months, I had
a chance to find out.

It took a while to get used to living in a building over-
looking the Vatican as well as a monument to Victor
Emmanuel; it took a while to become familiar with both

the solemnity of the papal ceremonies in St. Peter's and the fervor of the demonstrations in Piazza Venezia; it took a while to feel at home in a city where piety and violence rival each other in their intensity; and it took a while to take for granted that the devout worshipers in St. Peter's Square are as much a part of Roman life as the bohemians on the Piazza Navona. But after a month, the imposing buildings, the large crowds, and the sensational events seemed little more than the milieu for something much less visible but much more penetrating.

During these five months in Rome it wasn't the red cardinals or the Red Brigade who had the most impact on me, but the little things that took place between the great scenes. I met a few students of the San Egidio community "wasting" their time with grade-school dropouts and the elderly. I met a Medical Mission sister dedicating all her time to two old women who had become helpless and isolated in their upstairs rooms in Trastevere. I met young men and women picking up the drunks from the streets during the night and giving them a bed and some food. I met a priest forming communities for the handicapped. I met a monk who with three young Americans had started a contemplative community in one of Rome's suburbs. I met a woman so immersed in the divine mysteries that her face radiated God's love. I met many holy men and women offering their lives to others with a disarming generosity. And slowly, I realized that in the great circus of Rome, full of lion tamers and trapeze artists whose dazzling feats claim our attention, the real and true story was told by the clowns.

Clowns are not in the center of the events. They appear between the great acts, fumble and fall, and make us smile again after the tensions created by the heroes we came to admire. The clowns don't have it together, they do not succeed in what they try to do, they are awkward, out of balance, and left-handed, but . . . they are on our side. We respond to them not with admiration but with sympathy, not with amazement but with understanding, not with tension but with a smile. Of the virtuosi we say, "How can they do it?" Of the clowns we say, "They are like us." The clowns remind us with a tear and a smile that we share the same human weaknesses. Thus it is not surprising that pastoral psychologists such as Heije Faber in Holland and Seward Hiltner in the United States have found in the clown a powerful image to help us understand the role of those who choose to care and minister in contemporary society.

The longer I was in Rome, the more I enjoyed the clowns, those peripheral people who by their humble, saintly lives evoke a smile and awaken hope, even in a city terrorized by kidnapping and street violence. It is simplistic to think of the Church in Rome as an unimaginative bureaucracy, or a rigid bulwark of conservatism, or a splendid museum of Renaissance art. There are too many clowns in Rome, both inside and outside the Vatican, who contradict this view. I even came to feel that behind the black, purple, and red in the Roman churches and behind the suits and ties in the Roman offices there is enough clownishness left to give us hope.

It is this hope that underlies the four chapters of this book. They were written as lectures for English-speaking sisters, priests, and seminarians in Rome, but they may be read by others who journey spiritually, because they call attention to four clownlike elements in the spiritual life: solitude, celibacy, prayer, and contemplation. My growing love for the clowns in Rome made me desire to clown around a little myself and to speak about such foolish things as being alone, treasuring emptiness, standing naked before God, and simply seeing things for what they are. I came to feel that in this full, imposing, venerable, and busy city there must be a very deep desire to live out the other side of our being, the side that wants to play, dance, smile, and do many other "useless" things.

Sisters busy with many administrative responsibilities wanted to know about solitude. Seminarians already sensing the dangers of a lonely existence wondered about celibacy as a way of life. Priests aware of the heavy demands of a life of caring and ministry questioned the possibility of a prayerful life. And all those who went to class at one or another of the Roman universities and became more and more involved in the political, social, and cultural life of the city doubted if they would ever be able to satisfy their need for solitude and contemplation.

I have called this book *Clowning in Rome* because all the

subjects I was asked to talk about seemed to belong to the periphery of the world with which the newspapers *Il Messaggero* and *Il Corriere della Sera* fill their pages. At the same time the questions being asked are quite central to the life of the Spirit. The four chapters do not follow each other in a logical order, so one can read them independently. What binds them together is that they were inspired by Rome and written initially for people living there. I have since realized how universal these themes are and how all people on a spiritual journey might profit from this reflection. The specific place and audience color the context and give the book a somewhat bumpy character. But when clowning in Rome becomes a smooth performance, there won't be much left to evoke a smile.

CHAPTER ONE

SOLITUDE AND COMMUNITY

INTRODUCTION

When we reflect on current events we realize that our world is in a continuous state of emergency. Recently in Rome a judge was killed, and Aldo Moro, the leader of the Democrazia Cristiana, was kidnapped, while five of his bodyguards were assassinated. In Turin a police officer was shot to death, and in Milan two young leftist students were murdered. In Holland, Moluccan terrorists seized a government building and held the country in fear for many hours. In Israel, Palestinian guerrillas killed thirty-four bus passengers, and in Lebanon, hundreds of men, women, and children lost their lives in reprisal actions. In Rhodesia, Ethiopia, and Somalia, a state of war continues after many negotiations. In the United States and many other countries, strikes threaten the economy and reveal deep discontent about living conditions among millions of people. In Belgrade, a world conference on human rights failed to come to any significant agreements, while more violations are reported from the Soviet Union, Argentina, Paraguay, and other countries. The relationships among the main powers of the world are deteriorating, while the chances for a universal holocaust are increasing with the buildup of nuclear arsenals. And so, as we approach the end of the second millennium of the Christian era, our world is clouded with an all-pervading fear, a growing sense of despair, and a paralyzing awareness that indeed humanity has come to the verge of suicide.

We no longer have to ask ourselves if we are approaching a state of emergency. We are in the midst of it, right here and now, and we expect the future to mirror the past.

You do not have to be a great prophet to say that coming decades will most likely see not only more wars, more hunger, and more oppression, but also desperate attempts to escape them all. We have to be prepared for a period in which suicide will be as widespread as drugs, in which new types of zealots will roam the country frightening the people with announcements of things to come, and in which many new exotic cults with intricate rituals will try to ward off a final catastrophe. We have to be prepared for an outburst of new religious movements using Christ's name for the most un-spiritual practices. In short, we have to be prepared to live in a world in which fear, suspicion, mutual distrust, hatred, physical and mental torture, and an increasing confusion darken the hearts of millions of people.

It is in the midst of this dark world that we are invited to live and radiate hope. Is it possible? Can we become light, salt, and leaven to our brothers and sisters in the human family? Can we offer hope, courage, and confidence to the people of this era? Do we dare break through our paralyzing fear? Will people be able to say of us, "See how they love each other, how they serve their neighbor, and how they pray to their Lord?" Or do we have to confess that at this juncture of history we just do not have the needed strength or the generosity? How can we live in hope so as to give hope? And how do we find true joy?

When you asked me to reflect on solitude, I realized that I could only speak about it in the context of these urgent questions facing us today. It would be easy, and therefore tempting, simply to speak about the relationship between solitude and community in general, but that would not call you to the urgency of the situation. So I will try to explain how the state of the world in which we live has the potential to open our hearts to a new understanding of the depth and beauty of solitude in the lives of the serious seekers today.

I hope to talk about our lives as individuals, as families, and communities (both religious and secular) under three headings, namely: intimacy ("see how they love each other"), ministry ("see how they serve each other"), and prayer ("see how they pray to their Lord"), because these are life-giving forces that help us heal and become healers. Furthermore, I'll try to make the connection between solitude and obedience to the Spirit, solitude and purity of heart, and solitude and simplicity. I hope to show how these three aspects of our communal life and witness are connected with celibacy, obedience, and poverty and how they require a deep commitment to solitude.

SOLITUDE AND INTIMACY
The forces of fear and anger

How can solitude help our world? How can we, by practicing solitude, bring love into the world? In our emergency-oriented society, fear and anger have become powerful forces. Not only do we see in the daily newspapers people driven together by fear or bound together by anger, but we also start to realize that many of us in our families and communities are plagued by a restlessness tainted by fear and anger. We search to satisfy a growing need for community that offers a sense of belonging, a place where frustrations can be expressed, disappointments shared, and pains healed. We who in the past felt quite secure and self-confident today suffer from self-doubt, and sometimes from a deep sense of powerlessness. We who for years felt quite content in our choice of vocation are questioning the meaning of our life choices, wondering if our lives are valuable for others. We may even wonder if we are tainted by dubious motives and false aspirations, and we certainly ask ourselves whether or not we ever make truly free decisions.

This context of self-doubt leads to a deep sense of alienation and loneliness that has challenged us to develop new, more comfortable lifestyles within our own cultures and communities. Here we are discovering how deep our real needs are and how hard it is to feel satisfied in our own homes. It is not surprising that deep yearnings for affection, friendship, and intimacy, which until now had remained beneath the threshold of our consciousness, come to take their place in the very center of awareness. We are troubled and pained in the areas of sexuality, freedom, responsibility, guilt, and shame. These painful yearnings push us to desire a total break with the past and to seek new forms of intimacy that can be more directly experienced. Often those of us who are most sensitive to the fear and anger of our world seek most intensely for solutions, but we also experience deeply a need for affection and tenderness that no family or community can satisfy. This need is troubling and painful.

Thus we wonder if the fear and anger of our world have made it impossible for us to be like children playing pipes and inviting others to dance (Lk. 7:32). Inner torments and restlessness have reached such an intensity that our primary concern has become our own physical and emotional survival. This concern depletes our energy, so that a vital and convincing witness to God's loving and caring presence is hardly possible.

All this suggests that when there is no real intimacy in our lives we are unable to experience a safe and happy environment for very long in our fearful and angry world. For this reason we will take a very careful look at the importance of solitude in our lives. It might be that by de-emphasizing solitude in favor of the urgent needs of our world, we have endangered the very basis of our lives as Christian witnesses. Hence I would like first to discuss solitude as the source of a lasting sense of intimacy.

Free from compulsions

Solitude is the place where we can connect with profound bonds that are deeper than the emergency bonds of fear and anger. Although fear and anger indeed drive us together, they do not give rise to our love for one another. In solitude we come to the realization that we are not driven together but brought together. In solitude we come to know our fellow human beings not as partners who satisfy our deepest needs, but as brothers and sisters with whom we are called to give visibility to God's all-embracing love. In solitude we discover that family or community is not some common ideology but a response to a common call. In solitude we indeed experience that community is not made but given.

Solitude, then, is not private time in contrast to time together, nor is it a time to restore our tired minds. Solitude is very different from a "time-out" from our busy lives. Solitude is the very ground from which community grows. Whenever we pray alone, study, read, write, or simply spend quiet time away from the places where we interact with each other directly, we are potentially opened for a deeper intimacy with each other. It is a fallacy to think that we grow closer to each other only when we talk, play, or work together. Much growth certainly occurs in such human interactions, but these interactions derive their fruit from solitude, because in solitude our intimacy with each other is deepened. In solitude we discover each other in a way that physical presence makes difficult if not impossible. In solitude we know a bond with each other that does not depend on words, gestures, or actions but is rather a bond much deeper than our own efforts could ever create.

If we base our life together on our physical proximity, on our ability to spend time together, speak with each other, eat together, and worship together, life quickly starts fluctuating according to moods, personal attractiveness, and mutual compatibility, and thus becomes very demanding and tiring. Solitude, on the other hand, puts us in touch with a unity that precedes all unifying activities. In solitude we become aware that we were together before we came together and that life is not a creation of our will but rather an obedient response to the reality of our being united. Whenever we enter into solitude, we witness to a love that transcends our interpersonal communications and proclaims that we love each other because we have been loved first (1 Jn. 4:19). Solitude keeps us in touch with the sustaining love from which we draw strength. It sets us free from the compulsions of fear and anger and allows us to be in the midst of an anxious and violent world as a sign of hope and a source of courage. In short, solitude creates that free community, that natural family that makes bystanders say, "See how they love each other."

A chaste love

This view of solitude as fertile ground has very practical implications. It means that time for silence, individual reflection, and prayer are as important as acting together, working together, playing together, and worshiping together.

I am deeply convinced that gentleness, tenderness, peacefulness, and the inner freedom to move closer to each other, or to withdraw from each other, are nurtured in solitude. Without solitude we begin to cling to each other; we begin to worry about what we think and feel about each other; we quickly become suspicious of each other or irritated with each other; and we begin, often in unconscious ways, to scrutinize each other with a tiring hypersensitivity. Without solitude, shallow conflicts easily grow deep and cause painful wounds. Then "talking things out" becomes a burdensome obligation and daily life becomes so self-conscious that long-term living together is painful and almost impossible. Without solitude, we will always suffer from a gnawing question about more or less: "Does he love me more than she does? Is our love today less than it was yesterday?" These questions easily lead to divisions, tensions, apprehensions, and mutual irritability.

With solitude, however, we learn to depend on God, who calls us together in love, in whom we can rest, and through whom we can enjoy and trust each other even when our ability to express ourselves to each other is limited. With solitude, we are protected against the harmful effects of mutual suspicions, and our words and actions become more joyful expressions of an already existing trust, rather than a subtle way of asking for proof of trustworthiness. With solitude we can experience each other as different manifestations of a love that transcends all of us.

Solitude has an impact on the way we live our sexuality as well. Solitude prevents us from relating to our sexuality as a way to prove that we can love, and it liberates us from the compulsive quality of our neediness. Solitude allows us to experience our sexual feelings as yearnings for unconditional love and communion. In solitude we more easily find a free response to our sexual identity. Even sexual abstinence becomes a real option for men and women dedicated to the spiritual life.

For all of us solitude becomes the place where chastity finds its roots. Chastity obviously means much more than sexual abstinence. It is the gentle guide to all forms of intimacy. Living chastly opens us to the intimate knowledge of God's affective love for us and sets us free to develop creative relationships in our world without being caught up by the many "oughts" and "musts." Chastity makes intimacy more possible by freeing us from worldly compulsiveness.

And so solitude is essential to our lives because it liberates us from the powers of fear and anger and brings us to a sense of intimacy that transcends the emergencies of our present-day world. It offers us hope, because it calls us to look at each other and to say with a new amazement: "See how we are loving one another."

SOLITUDE AND CARING
The individualization of the caring ministries

How does solitude also strengthen the communal witness of service? One of the most obvious responses to an emergency situation is that we give up our long-range goals and focus on the most pressing problems. When a city or town is being bombed, doctors stop their research on complex medical problems and give first-aid to the wounded. When a sense of emergency begins to pervade a culture, short-term solutions, provisional care, and temporary aid easily obscure the need for carefully studied long-term projects.

I wonder if much of our service to and care of each other in our families and neighborhoods has not been deeply affected by this sense of emergency. Forms of caring to which many of us were committed for decades have suddenly lost their appeal, and we have no energy for them. Teaching, hospital work, and many other traditional forms of community service no longer seem to be responses to the urgent needs of the times, because our lives are so filled with business and distraction. Life is frenetic and stressful. In the midst of our nagging desire for relevance, we are overcome with our own need to keep moving, often "running on empty." The questions "How are you doing individually?" or "How are you faithful to your calling in life?" are often difficult to answer. Mostly we respond by saying "I work in a hospital," or "I teach in a school," or "I work in a professional setting, in a parish, or in an individual job, and I try to support others while raising a family or living in community." Our responses indicate that the urgency of work takes precedence over the state of our being.

There is a wide variety of ministries now available: to

prisoners, to drug addicts, to shut-ins, to marginalized people; ministries in parishes, in factories, in mental institutions; also ministries that focus on music, art, or the media. The deinstitutionalization of religious life has opened up an enormous range of ministerial options that, not too long ago, were practically taboo for many ordinary men and women.

But there is also a loss, and that is the loss of the communal character of Christian ministry. Often it seems that our ministries have become so individualized that it has become very hard to offer convincing visibility to our communal efforts to care. The emphasis on the particular talents of the individuals has made it very hard sometimes to speak about a ministry held in common. Often we can only speak about the ministries of individual members, which is good but lacks the power of being together.

I wonder if, by this individualization, we have not lost the possibility of being a common witness. As families, parishes and religious communities, we not only desire to serve individuals, our neighbors, and others in need, but we also yearn to share our conviction and hope, with courage and confidence, with the larger society. Precisely in a culture so ripped apart by emergencies, it is not enough to care for the many wounded individuals; it is also urgent to offer hope to the many who are not directly touched by us, but who see our common life and say: "See how they serve their neighbor." The great power of a common vocation is that by its special visibility as a communal calling it can touch, heal, and inspire many more than those who are directly affected by it.

> *Personally I have found enormous strength in the witness of the Taizé community although I have never been there. I have found great hope in the work of Jean Vanier although I have never met him. I have found much comfort in just knowing about the work and life of the Little Brothers and Little Sisters, the Missionaries of Charity, and the San Egidio Community. These communal ministries give hope to our world and prevent us from joining the many pessimistic voices which de-energize us.*

It is the working together that is so crucial in our time and needs to be of great concern to us.

A common vocation

What has all this to do with solitude? Solitude is the place where we find our identity. It is the place where we take a few moments in quiet before God to see who we are in relationship to God and to each other. In solitude we listen and wait to "hear" the voice of the One who loves us and who calls us to deeper love. Why, you might ask, is this the case?

Solitude is the place where we are with God and God alone, and where we can come to understand our own most individual call. And, we are never called alone. We are always called together. In solitude we recognize how we put our most personal talents in the service of a common work. It is very naïve to think that our individual giftedness can be directly translated into a call. To say, I can write well, so God wants me to be a writer; I can teach well, so God wants me to be a teacher; I can play the piano well, so God wants me to be a pianist, makes us forget that our own self-understanding is not necessarily God's understanding of us. There was a time in which a one-sided view of humility led to the negation or denial of individual gifts. Hopefully, that time is gone. But to think that individual gifts are the manifestation of God's will reveals a one-sided view of calling and obscures the fact that our talents can be as much the way to God as *in the way of* God.

In solitude we take some distance from the many opinions and ideas of those around us and become vulnerable to God. In solitude we listen carefully to the voice of love encouraging us to distinguish between our desires and our tasks, between our urges and our vocation, between the cravings of our heart and the call of God. I have the sense that when solitude is not an integral part of daily life we quickly become deaf to God's loving voice, mostly concerned with doing "my thing," and without much thought about our communal responsibility. At that point the family or the community is little more than a mutual support group in which our awareness of our common call has moved to the background of our consciousness.

Solitude is the place where our common call becomes apparent. We should never forget that God calls us as a people, and that our individual vocations should always be seen as a part of the larger vocation of the family or the community. We cannot use the group solely as a means to develop or give shape to our individual aspirations. As long as we see the community as a support system to help us realize our individual ideals, we are more children of our time than children of God. Our own individual calling can only be seen as a particular manifestation of the calling of the community to which we belong.

A few quiet moments in solitude is the ground where our common calling as family becomes manifest. In that sacred moment we empty ourselves of our needs for self-affirmation, self-realization, and self-fulfillment and begin to experience how God's call comes to us through the people with whom we live. The deep love we have for each other leads us to the conviction that our life of love is expressed in the caring for each other and for brothers and sisters everywhere.

The obedient family community

This view of solitude—as the place where our common aspirations as a body are realized—has some very concrete implications. It implies that listening to God's call is central to the whole group and cannot be reduced simply to individuals at random or left as the sole responsibility of the parents or of the authority figure. Obedience is about an experience of real listening to God. We do that in solitude, alone or together. We have experienced how difficult it is to listen, because there seems to be an urgency to talk and to solve outstanding questions. But listening to human experience is not so simple. To do it well we need some space and time alone, or alone together, in solitude. This allows us to be more open and more sensitive to the ways God calls us to be together for others.

Silence and solitude do not attract us when we are busy and preoccupied. Thus we have to structure some short periods of time when we can be alone, together. Being alone with God for yourself is a very different experience from being alone with God as part of your life together. I am deeply convinced that great renewal will develop wherever we enter into solitude together to discover how God is calling us. No important decision, no important change in direction should be made without periods of long, silent listening in which all members are participating in some way.

I might also mention the importance of making regular times of silence. Silence imposed can be very, very fruitless—but silence as the way in which we listen together to God's presence in our midst and open ourselves to God's loving guidance is indispensable in relationships. There is so much emphasis on words in the media, newspapers, study days, and sharing sessions that it seems important to deepen our realization that words can only bear fruit when they are born in silence. We will also discover that in periods of

crises, conflicts, and strong emotional tensions, silence not only
offers healing but also shows new ways forward in our life together.

Solitude, then, is the quiet place of listening. The contemporary community, especially in a time of emergency, must meet and adapt to constant changes in people and in the world around it, so a deep commitment to solitude in this context makes a lot of sense. We might practically judge the state of our psychological and emotional health by our practice of solitude. Our ability to care in a world of ongoing change grows when it is deeply rooted in a quiet, silent encounter with our faithful God. This allows us to move through our days without being terribly disturbed and distraught by the interruptions or disruptions. It also allows us to perform a diversity of concrete tasks without haste and distraction. In solitude we re-find our center and rediscover that our unity is continually strengthened and nurtured.

Together, as we deepen our personal relationship with the God who is calling us to care, it will then be possible to live in an emergency-oriented world, responding creatively to the concrete events of the day without being seduced into panic reactions or erratic movements. Our solitude prevents the emergencies from throwing us back on ourselves in self-protective or self-serving actions and urges us to give hope to one another. We are called to be a sign of love in the world that causes people to say with amazement: "See how they serve their neighbor."

SOLITUDE AND PRAYER
Religious secularism

Just as solitude affects our mutual love and our common caring, so too has solitude a deep influence on our relationship with the God who calls us beloved. Our lives, individually and together, as well as our caring not only make people say: "See how they love each other," and "See how they serve, support, and care for their neighbors," but also "See how they seem to know and love the Lord!"

It is very simplistic to say that emergencies make us pay more attention to God and reawaken in us our desire to trust in God and to pray. Because of fear and anger the opposite is more often true. The pressures of living in our society make us react to questions and problems more with bitterness, resentment, and even hatred. Far from being inspired, we seem to have forgotten about God. We are cynical about so much suffering in ourselves and in the world and we do not know how to integrate that with our spiritual aspirations. As in a love-hate relationship, feelings of deep disillusionment color our capacity to relate with the One we once accepted and tried to follow. We feel ambivalent and dissatisfied, wondering if God can really be trusted and if God really is a personal God who is "close to the brokenhearted."

We aren't questioning this with words, but our behavior betrays us. We say to a friend, "I will pray for you." But we walk away without any sense of a commitment to pray because we have doubts about prayers being answered. We listen to sermons and homilies affirming the benefits of a life of communion with God, but somewhere deep down we really believe that it is action, not prayer, that will satisfy our needs. We may think prayer is good when there is nothing more important to do, but we have strong reservations and doubts about God's effectiveness in our world or God's personal interest in us. We are no longer conscious of *God-with-us.*

I encounter friends and colleagues who are plagued by deep, hostile feelings toward God without having any way to express or work with them. I don't meet many people today who live only for God.

Since we speak of our time as the secular age, shouldn't we be willing to accept that secularism has entered deeply into our own hearts, leaving us with hesitations, suspicions, angers, and hatreds that have corroded our friendship with God?

In many if not most of our lives, communion with God in prayer has lost its central place, not only because of changing conditions in our society but also because God seems to have become a very dubious partner. The Lord seems to be someone with whom we *have* to relate to avoid problems but whose presence has little or no effect on our lives. Although for many of us these feelings and experiences linger on the threshold of consciousness, some of us experience ourselves as cowards who lack the courage to forget about God and get on with our lives. This feeling of cowardice reveals itself to us in the sense of being "caught" by God in a net of fear and dependency. It is painful and can make us feel angry and unfree.

In many of our homes, God is little more than a silver frame with a picture or a crucifix on the wall. Beautiful liturgies, insightful books and conferences, as well as occasional retreats and celebrations that used to be inspiring no longer inspire or touch us in the same way, and somewhere deep down we know we can live without them.

It is, therefore, not surprising that many people have left their religious communities and their partners rather easily, with the sensation that emotional as well as physical chains have been taken away, allowing them to do better what they did well before. All this is not meant as an indictment. On the contrary, consumerism and secularism have entered so deeply into our way of being in the world that it cannot be subject to simple accusations. But it can be made subject to reflection, because it shows how we have become so much a part of our emergency-oriented world and explains why it is difficult for contemporary religious communities and parishes to be unambiguous witnesses to the living God.

The great encounter

It is precisely in this context of our feeling caught and frustrated that solitude has its deepest meaning. Solitude is the place where *God-with-us* can be unpacked and where we connect with the *God Who is our Origin*, our loving and benevolent Father and Mother, our Savior, our unconditional Lover. And solitude is the place where our own hearts uncover our deep yearning to be loved unconditionally, and to love with our whole beings. Solitude is indeed the place of the great encounter, from which all other encounters derive their meaning. In solitude we meet the *One Who calls us beloved*. In solitude, we leave behind our many activities, concerns, plans, and projects, opinions, and convictions to enter into the presence of Love, naked, vulnerable, open, and receptive. Here we encounter a Father/Mother God who is all love, all care, all forgiveness. In solitude we are led to a personal and intimate relationship with Love itself.

I am not saying this to suggest that there is an easy solution to our ambivalent relationship with God. Solitude is not a solution but a *direction*. The echo of this direction is heard in the prophet Elijah, who did not find Yahweh in the mighty wind, or the earthquake, or the fire, but in the still, small voice. Jesus points in this direction too by going early in the mornings to the mountain to be in communion with his Father.

Every time we enter into solitude we withdraw from our windy, tornadolike, fiery lives and we open ourselves for the great encounter, the meeting with Love. But first in our solitude is the discovery of our own restlessness, our drivenness, our compulsiveness, our urge to act quickly, to make an impact, and to have influence. We really have to try very hard to withstand the gnawing urge to return as quickly as possible to the work of "relevance." But when we persevere with the help of a gentle discipline, we slowly come to hear the still, small voice and to feel the delicate breeze, and so come to know the presence of Love. This love goes straight to the heart, making us see the truth of who we really are. We are God's beloved children.

Right here we are connected to the greatest gift of solitude. It is the gift of a true self, a true identity. Solitude leads us to a new intimacy with each other and makes us see our common task precisely because in solitude we come to know our true nature, our true self, our true identity. That knowledge of who we really are allows us to live and work with each other in community. As long as our life and our work together are based on a false or distorted self-understanding, we are bound to become entangled in inter-personal conflicts and lose perspective on our common task.

This leads us to take another look at our fear and anger. While fear and anger are the most natural and obvious reactions to a state of emergency, they can be unmasked as expressions of our false selves. When we are trembling with fear or seething with anger, we have sold ourselves to the world or to a false God. Fear and anger take our freedom away and make us victims of the strong seductions of our world. Fear, as well as anger, when we look at them in solitude and quiet, reveal to us how deeply our sense of worth is dependent either on our success in the world or on the opinions of others. We suddenly realize that we have become what we do or what others think of us.

In solitude, however, the two pervasive forces of fear and anger lose their power to the embrace of a loving God. That is what Saint John means when he says: "In love there can be no fear, but fear is driven out by perfect love" (1 Jn. 4:18). In solitude we are gradually led to the truth that we are God's creation, work of God's hand, beloved sons and daughters, loved and held in the heart of God.

Thus solitude is a place of transformation. When we find space and silence we are transformed from people who need to show all that we have acquired and all the wonderful things we do, into people who raise our open and empty hands to a loving God, recognizing that our life and all we have is a free gift from God.

In solitude, we not only encounter God but come to know ourselves in our truth. We come to know God as Father and Mother and we recognize the true beauty of who we really are. To the degree that we know God and know ourselves as children of God, we come to find each other not as a group of individuals huddling together out of fear or driven together by common anger, but as a community of people, bound by a common heritage. As such we are called to freely witness to the One who made us and who is present in our midst.

Empty before God

When we see solitude as the place of an intimate encounter, the place where we commune with God as the loving Father and Mother, then we know that solitude is the sacred meeting place, where we are truly ourselves. Prayer is the breath of life both for us and for the Christian community. With a superficial sense of God and mistaken self-identity, real communion is not possible, nor is real community possible. The lie suffocates us and our life together.

In this final section I would like to emphasize the importance of our solidarity with the whole human family. If it is true that solitude diverts us from our fear and anger and makes us empty for a relationship with God, then it is also true that our emptiness provides a very large and sacred space where we can welcome all the people of the world. There is a powerful connection between our emptiness and our ability to welcome. When we give up what sets us apart from others—not just property but also opinions, prejudices, judgments, and mental preoccupations—then we have room within to welcome friends as well as enemies. When we pray for others, we invite them to enter with us into our solitude and there we lift them up to the God we encounter. In true solitude there is unlimited space for others because we are empty. In this poverty nobody stands over and against us, because our enemy is only our enemy as long as we have something to defend. But when we have nothing to hold onto or protect, when we have nothing we consider exclusively ours, then nobody will threaten us. Rather, in the center of our solitude we meet all men and women as brothers and sisters. In true solitude, we stand so naked and so vulnerable before God, and we become so deeply aware of our total dependency on God's love, that not only our friends but also those who kill, lie, torture, rape, and wage wars become part of our very flesh and blood. Yes, in true solitude we are so totally empty and poor that we find our solidarity with brothers and sisters everywhere. Our hearts, full of God and empty of fear and anger, become a welcoming home for God and for our whole human family on earth. So bringing our brothers and sisters into our solitude and prayer by praying for them is a choice of self-emptying, inviting us to give up all that divides us from others to *become* those we pray for so that God may touch them in us.

CONCLUSION

This brings me to the conclusion of this reflection on the relationship between solitude and a life lived in a community or a family. Let me now summarize.

First of all, I have tried to demonstrate how deeply the state of emergency of our world has affected our lives as family members, parishioners, and religious. Our interpersonal relationships have been tainted by fear and anger, our common tasks have been threatened by fragmentation and individualization, and our life of prayer has lost its central place in our daily lives together. Secondly, I have pointed to the practice of solitude not as the simple solution to these problems but as a place from where a response to the emergencies of our time can be made. I have described solitude as the place for a wonderful encounter with God, as the place where mature intimacy develops among people, and as the place where we discover or rediscover our common calling to be children of the same Father and Mother. I have tried to show that solitude is the foundation of our life together in the family, the parish, and the community. Finally, I wanted to help you see how deepening our solitude offers a context for a new perspective on the contemporary meaning of chastity, obedience, and poverty. Solitude makes us experience God's love as the source of all human love and thus makes us see that chastity is the guide for our intimate relationships with each other. Solitude makes us obedient to the call of God to a communal life, and solitude asks us to become poor and so to create a free space where all the suffering people in the world can be received and lifted up in unceasing prayer. Thus solitude is the ground on which chastity, obedience, and poverty can blossom and become rich gifts for our lives together.

I hope that I have been able to convince you of the

indispensability of solitude in the life of the family, the parish, and the religious community. At the end of the present millennium, let us deepen our commitment to solitude so that, surrounded by many apocalyptic events, we will give visibility to God's faithfulness. Let us be true to our identity and thus lead many people to the hopeful observations "See how they love each other; see how they serve their neighbor; see how they pray to their Lord."

CELIBACY AND THE HOLY

INTRODUCTION

When we look out over the city of Rome, walk in its streets, or ride in its buses, we quickly realize that it is a crowded city full of houses, full of people, full of cars, yes—even full of cats! We see men and women moving quickly in all directions, we hear joyful and angry voices mixed with a great variety of street sounds, we smell many odors—especially cappuccino—and we feel the Italian embrace by which we gain a friend or lose our money. It is a busy, congested city, in which life manifests itself in all its boisterous intensity. But in the midst of this lively and colorful conglomeration of houses, people, and cars, there are the domes of Rome pointing to the places set apart for the Holy. The churches of Rome are like beautiful frames around empty spaces witnessing to the One who is the quiet, still, center of all human life. The churches are not useful, not practical, not requiring immediate action or quick response. They are spaces without loud noises, hungry movements, or impatient gestures. They are tranquil spaces, strangely empty most of the time. Their presence speaks of something different from the hustle and bustle around them. They are not museums. They call and invite us to be silent, to sit or kneel, to listen attentively, and to rest with our whole being.

A city without these carefully protected, empty spaces where one can bask in the silence from which all words grow, and where one can rest in the stillness from which all actions flow, is in danger of losing its real center.

I believe that this busy city with its many quiet places offers us an image of the meaning of celibacy in our contemporary society. After all, doesn't the active street life represent that part of us that wants to be with others, to move and to produce? And isn't the dome, carefully protecting the empty church, an image of that other part of us that needs to be protected and even defended to prevent us from losing our bearings? Our inner sanctum, that inner, holy place, that sacred center in our lives where only God may enter, is as important for our lives as the domes are for the city of Rome.

Much can be said about celibacy, but in this reflection I simply want to reflect on it from one perspective. I want to look at celibacy as a witness to the rich and deep inner life of our hearts and of our spirits. By giving special visibility to this inner sanctum where God's Spirit makes a home in us, I wish to affirm and proclaim that all human intimacy finds its deepest meaning and fulfillment when it is experienced and lived as a participation in the intimacy of God alone. The celibate man or woman proclaims this hope by recognizing, receiving, and living the gift of celibacy.

To explore the meaning of this incredible witness of the celibate life, I will focus on three domains: on the world in which celibacy is chosen and lived, on the nature of the witness that the celibate person offers to this world, and finally, on the choice of lifestyle that enhances and strengthens the witness.

THE WORLD IN WHICH CELIBACY IS CHOSEN AND LIVED
The limits of the interpersonal

The world in which celibacy wants to be a witness for a holy, empty space is a world that puts great emphasis on interpersonal relationships. We can safely say that in the Western culture of the last few decades the value of coming together, being together, living together, and loving together has received more attention than ever before. The healing power of eye contact, of attentive listening, and of the careful touch has been explored by many psychologists, sensitivity trainers, and communication experts. Practically every year you can hear about a new type of therapy, a new form of consciousness enlarging, or a new method of communication. Many, many people suffering from feelings of isolation, alienation, or loneliness find new hope and strength in these experiments in togetherness. Just seeing the great popularity and the growing influence of reevaluation therapy is enough to convince a sympathetic observer that a deep need is being responded to.

We indeed need each other and are able to give each other much more than we often realize. Too long have we been burdened by fear and guilt, and too long have we denied each other the affection and closeness we rightly desire. We, therefore, have much to learn from those who are trying to open up new and more creative interpersonal relations.

But critical questions still need to be raised. Can real intimacy be reached without a deep respect for that holy space within and between us, that space that should remain untouched by human hands? Can human intimacy really be fulfilling when every space within and between us is being filled up? Is the emphasis on the healing possibilities of human togetherness often the result of a one-sided perception of our human predicament? These questions have a new urgency in this time of human-potential movements. I often wonder if we do not think or feel that our painful experience of loneliness is primarily a result of our lack of interpersonal closeness. We seem to think: "If I could just break through my fear to express my real feelings of love and hostility, I could hold my head up. If I could just feel free to hold a friend, or if I could just talk honestly and openly with my own people, I would be so much more fulfilled. If I could just live with someone who really cares . . . then I would have again some inner peace and experience again some inner wholeness." When we have these thoughts, we feel a certain relief, but the question still remains whether or not the real source of our healing and wholeness can be found.

Because traditional patterns of human communications have broken down and family, profession, and neighborhood no longer offer the intimate bonds and the security of the past, the basic human condition of aloneness has entered very deeply into our emotional awareness. We constantly feel tempted to want more from those around us than they can give. We relate to our neighbors with the hope and the supposition that they are able to fulfill most of our deepest needs, and then we find ourselves disillusioned, angry, and frustrated when they do not. We know that when we expect a friend or lover to take away our deepest pain, we expect from him or her something that cannot be given by another human being. We have heard that no human being can understand us fully, or give us unconditional love, or offer constant affection that enters into the core of our being and heals our deepest brokenness. We know this in our heads but our loneliness pushes us to expect it anyway. When we forget this profound truth and expect of others more than they can give, we are quickly disillusioned and we easily become resentful, bitter, revengeful, and even violent.

Lately we have become very much aware of the fragile border between intimacy and violence. We see or hear about cruelty between husband and wife, parents and children, brothers and sisters, and we realize that those who desire so desperately to be loved often find themselves entangled in violent relationships. The stories in the daily paper about sexual aggression, mutilation, and murder evoke a vision of people desperately grasping each other and clinging to each other, crying out and shouting for love, but not receiving anything but more violence.

Spinoza's words "Nature abhors a vacuum" seem quite applicable. The temptation is indeed very great to take flight into an intimacy and closeness that does not leave any open space. Much suffering results from this suffocating closeness.

With praying hands

I found a good image to describe our predicament in the book *Existential Metapsychiatry* by New York psychiatrist Thomas Hora.* He calls *personalism* the great emphasis on interpersonal relationships as the way to healing, and he compares this personalism with the interlocking fingers of two hands. The fingers of the two hands can intertwine only to the point that a stalemate is reached. After that, the only possible movement is backward, causing friction and eventually pain. And too much friction leads to separation. When we relate to each other as the interlocking fingers of two hands we enter into a suffocating closeness that does not leave any free space. When lonely people with a strong desire for intimacy move closer and closer to each other in the hope of coming to an experience of belonging and wholeness, all too frequently they find themselves locked in a situation in which closeness leads to friction, friction to pain, and pain to separation. Many relationships are so short-lived precisely because there is an intense desire for closeness and a minimal amount of space that allows for free movement. Because of the high emotional expectation with which we enter into a relationship, we often panic when we do not experience the inner contentment for which we had hoped. We may try very hard to alleviate our

Existential Metapsychiatry by Thomas Hora (New York: Seabury Press, 1977), p. 32.

tensions by exploring in much detail our life together, only to end up in a stalemate, tired, exhausted, and finally forced to separate in order to avoid mutual harm.

Thomas Hora suggests as the image for a true human relationship two hands coming together parallel in a prayerful gesture, pointing beyond themselves and moving freely in relation to each other. I find this a helpful image, exactly because it makes it clear that a mature human intimacy requires a deep and profound respect for the free and empty space that needs to exist within and between partners and that asks for continuous mutual protection and nurture. Only in this way can a relationship be lasting, precisely because mutual love is experienced as a participation in a greater and earlier love to which it points. In this way intimacy can be rich and fruitful, since it has been given carefully protected space in which to grow. This relationship no longer is a fearful clinging to each other but a free dance, allowing space in which we can move forward and backward, constantly form new patterns, and see each other as always new.

The world in which we live is a world with many fearful, lonely, anxious people clinging to each other to find some relief, some satisfaction, and some joy. The tragedy of our world is that much of the intense desire for love, acceptance, and belonging is cruelly turned into jealousy, resentment, and violence, often to the bitter surprise of those who had no other desire than to live in peace and love. In this world with many people anxiously clinging to each other, a sign of hope needs to be given. In this world, celibacy, as a visible manifestation of the holy space in an overcrowded world, can be a powerful witness in service of mature human relationships.

THE WITNESS
Vacancy for God

The best definition of celibacy, I think, is the definition of Thomas Aquinas, who calls celibacy a vacancy for God. To be a celibate means to be empty for God, to be free and open for God's presence, to be available for God's service. This view on celibacy, however, has often led to the false idea that being empty for God is a special privilege of celibates, while other people involved in all sorts of interpersonal relationships are not empty but full, occupied as well as preoccupied. If we look at celibacy as a state of life that upholds the importance of God's presence in our lives in contrast with other states of life that lead to entanglement in worldly affairs, we quickly slip into a dangerous elitism, considering celibates as domes rising up amidst the many low houses of the city.

I think that celibacy can never be considered a special prerogative of a few members of the people of God. Celibacy, in its deepest sense of creating and protecting emptiness for God, is an essential part of all forms of Christian life: marriage, friendship, single life, and community life. We will never fully understand what it means to be celibate unless we recognize that celibacy is, first of all, an element and even an essential element in the life of all Christians. Let me illustrate how this is true in marriage and friendship.

Marriage is not a lifelong attraction of two individuals to each other but a call for two people to witness together to God's love. The basis of marriage is not mutual affection, or feelings, or emotions and passions that we associate with love, but a calling, a vocation. It is to understand that we are elected to build together a house for God in this world. It is to be like the two cherubs whose outstretched wings sheltered the Ark of the Covenant and created a space where Yahweh could be present (Ex. 25: 10–12; 1 Ki. 8:6–7). Marriage is a relationship where man and woman protect and nurture the inner sanctum within and between them, and they witness to that by the way that they love each other. We often think the word *vocation* applies only to those called to religious life, but marriage is also a *vacare Deo*, a call of God. And celibacy is an important part of marriage. This is not simply because married couples may have to live separated from each other for long periods of time. Nor is it because they may need to abstain from sexual relations because of physical, mental, or spiritual reasons. It is rather that the intimacy of marriage itself is an intimacy that is based on the common participation in a love greater than the love that two people can offer each other. The real mystery of marriage is not that husband and wife love each other so much that they can recognize God in each other's lives, but more because God loves them so much that they can discover each other more and more as living reminders of God's divine presence. They are brought together, indeed, as two prayerful hands extended toward God and forming in this way a home for God in this world.

The same thing is true for friendship. Deep and mature friendship does not mean that we keep looking each other in the eyes, constantly impressed or enraptured by each other's beauty, talents, and gifts, but it does mean that together we look at the one who calls us to a life of service.

I was deeply impressed by the way the members of the San Egidio community in Trastevere described their relationships with each other. They made it very clear to me that friendship is very important to them, but that they have to learn in their apostolate to keep seeing their relationships with each other in the context of their common call. As soon as the relationship itself becomes central they are moving away from their vocation. They have to be willing to let new developments in their apostolates separate them from each other for certain periods of time, and they also have to be willing to see and experience their separations as an invitation to deepen their relationship with their first Love, the Lord, and then through the Spirit of the Lord with each other. That is why they feel so strongly that their weekly Eucharist and their daily vespers together strengthen them and nurture their love for each other.

Around the table and in praise together they find each other as friend, and they renew their commitment to each other. There they draw the courage to follow the Lord even when they are being asked by God to go in different directions. Thus their relationships are really a standing together around the altar or around the holy, empty space one sees in Rubler's icon of the Holy Trinity. Together the three figures are committed to protect the empty space in and between each other.

And so, every relationship carries within its center a holy vacancy, a space that is for the first Love, God alone. Without that holy center, partnership and friendship become like a city without domes to remind it of its center, a city without meaning or direction for all its activities.

Living reminders

Men and women dedicated in religious life often consecrate themselves by a vow of celibacy. This too has a very important place in our world. By choosing the consecrated life, a person declares a priority for the first Love Who is God. The celibate person is a witness and a sign, reminding others of their source and their goal.

We are the children of God first and we all belong to God first. Everyone does. Those who live consecrated celibacy do not attach themselves to one particular person, and by their lives they remind us that our relationship with God, as the children of God, is the beginning, the source, and the goal of all human relationships. By his or her life of nonattachment, the celibate lifts up this beautiful truth about our Christian life.

The celibate is like a clown in the circus who, between the scary acts of the trapeze artists and lion tamers, fumbles and falls, reminding us that no human activity is ultimately as important as the virtuosi make us believe. Celibates live out a holy emptiness by not marrying, by not trying to build for themselves a house or a fortune, by not trying to wield as much influence as possible, and by not filling their lives with events, people, or creations for which they will be remembered. The hope is that by their "empty" lives, God will be more readily recognized as the source of all human life and activity. Especially by not marrying and by abstaining from the most intimate expression of human love, the celibate becomes a living sign of the limits of interpersonal relationships and of the centrality of the inner sanctum that no human being may violate.

To whom, then, is the celibate's witness directed? I dare to say that celibacy is, first of all, a witness to men and women who are married. I wonder if we have explored enough the very important relationship between marriage and celibacy. Lately I have become aware of this interrelatedness in a very painful way, realizing that the crisis of celibate people and the crisis of married people happened simultaneously. At the same time that many priests and religious persons began to move away from the celibate life, I saw many couples questioning the value of their commitment to each other.

These two phenomena, although they are not directly connected with each other as cause and effect, are closely related, because marriage and celibacy are two entirely different ways of living within the Christian community and of supporting each other. The celibate person is a support to married people in their commitment to each other, because they are reminded by the celibate of their own "empty" center. Seeing the life of a celibate person, they know that they need to protect and nurture their sacred center and thus live a life that does not depend simply upon the stability of emotions and affections. Their lives as husband and wife are also to be rooted in their individual and common love for the One who called them together. And, married people witness to those who have chosen the celibate life, demonstrating how the love of God creates a family and an intimate community from rich and creative human relationships. Married people gift celibate people with a vision of how their love leads them to become fruitful, generous, affectionate, and faithful to their children and to others in need. Married people are a living reminder of the covenant that celibates live with God. Thus celibacy and marriage need each other.

Celibates can indeed have a very good understanding of married life and married people of celibate life. Remarks such as "You don't know what you are talking about because you are not married (or celibate)" are misleading. Precisely because marriage and celibacy are in each other's service and bound together by their common witness to God's love as the love from which all human loves originate, celibate and married people can be of invaluable help to each other by supporting their different lifestyles.

Celibate people not only witnesses to married people but also, together with married people, speak of the presence of God in the world to anyone who searches and listens. In a world so congested and so entangled in conflict and pain, celibates by their dedication to God in a single lifestyle, and married people by their dedication to God in a life together, are signs of God's goodness and love in this world. They both ask us in different ways to turn to God as the fountain and source of all human relationships. They both say in different ways that without giving God the first place in our hearts in the midst of the city, we will ultimately fail in the hopeless attempt to fabricate peace and love by ourselves. The celibate speaks of the need to respect the inner sanctum at all cost; the married person speaks of the need to base his or her relationships on intimacy first with God. But both speak for the Source of all love and for God's presence in the world. Together they give form to the beauty of the Christian community and they stand out as signs of hope in a world of alienation and loneliness.

Thus, as we regard our torn and suffering world and try

so hard to create better human relationships, celibacy speaks volumes about how those relationships might better be achieved. Let this encourage us and give us hope. Let us make real efforts to create space and time for the God who sent Jesus into the world to show us the way to love. Let us grow in the knowledge that we *can* love each other, even though it is difficult. We do this because we have been loved first with such abundance.

THE LIFESTYLE
Useless . . .

When we look at celibacy as a *vacare Deo*, a being empty for God as a visible witness for the life with God in the inner sanctum, then it becomes clear that sexual abstinence can never be the most important aspect of celibacy. Not being married or not being involved in a sexual relationship does not constitute the celibate life. Celibacy is an openness to God and sexual abstinence is only one of its manifestations. Celibacy is a lifestyle in which we try to witness to the priority of God in all relationships. This involves every part of our life: the way we eat and drink, work and play, sleep and rest, speak and remain silent. It is an openness to being loved first by God. The celibate life is bound to touch those we encounter because it is a sort of ongoing street theater constantly raising questions in people's minds about the deeper meaning of their own existence.

Two necessary supports of a celibate lifestyle nurture and protect this certain vacancy for God: contemplative prayer and voluntary poverty. Contemplative prayer is an essential element of the celibate life, because it is a constant experience of having space and being empty for God. Contemplative prayer is not a way of being busy with God instead of with people. It is more a response to God's ultimate desire to make a home in our hearts. Instead of business it calls us to become still and to wait for God without anything to show, to prove, or to argue. It is to stop, wait, and trust that God fills our emptiness. It can be painful, and it is certainly countercultural.

Thus, an intimate connection exists between celibacy and this prayer of waiting and listening and trusting. Both celibacy and contemplative prayer call us to be vacant for God. In our utilitarian culture, where we suffer from a collective compulsion to do something practical, helpful, or useful, and where we feel compelled to make a contribution that can give us a sense of our own worth, contemplative prayer is a form of radical criticism. It is not useful or practical. It is simply to waste time for and with God. It stops us in our busyness to remind all of us that our God is personal and caring, and thus creating and sustaining us on our incredible planet earth. To stand naked, powerless, and vulnerable before God, therefore, is a critical expression of the celibate lifestyle.

In this useless prayer, God comes to meet us. Our task

is to be empty, free, and open, conscious of *God-with-us*, sensing God present, listening with our hearts to the voice of love. Slowly we come to know the presence as Jesus did when he went to the hills early in the morning to rest in communion with his Father. The Lord comes to us in our emptiness and fills us with deep, intimate affection for God and for our brothers and sisters in the human family. So, we want to work hard to develop a very warm, affective, and intimate prayer life that allows time and space where the gentle, caring presence of our God actually touches us and influences the life we want to live. This communion with the Author of love gradually brings us to new freedom because we experience acceptance and belonging. We know in our encounter that we are not alone but that we live in the embrace of One whose fatherhood embodies motherly, brotherly, and sisterly love. Knowing such intimacy in prayer is the foundation of our life in this world, and we discover that we do not need to cling to other people for self-affirmation and affection. The abundance of God's love, present in us, is the source of all our ministry.

And poor . . .

Besides contemplative prayer, the celibate lifestyle also asks for voluntary poverty. A wealthy celibate is like a fat sprinter. Anyone who is serious about celibacy has to ask, "Am I poor?" If the answer is "No, I am much better off than most people because I can buy more than my parishioners, and eat and drink better than those to whom I minister," then we have not yet taken our celibacy seriously. The choice to live simply is probably one of the most striking signs of a celibate lifestyle. It is a fact that some people do not take celibacy seriously because they contrast their daily struggle to pay the bills for food, housing, and education with the carefree life of ministers and other celibates, and they wonder who is really living out the witness of the Gospel. If there is one aspect of contemporary ministry that needs emphasis today, it is voluntary simplicity of life. Each one of us is able to name the sins of capitalism and each day we hear about the millions of brothers and sisters who suffer from lack of food, shelter, and the most basic care. How can we consider ourselves a witness for the God who fills our emptiness when our own lives are cluttered with material possessions, our bellies overfull, and our minds crowded with worries about what to do with what we have? Voluntary poverty is probably the most necessary form of our vacancy for God in the world in which we live. It has to be the most convincing sign of our solidarity with the suffering in our human family, as well as a most powerful support for a life of sexual abstinence. Wherever there is vitality, in individuals or in the Churches, there is a certain poverty or emptiness. This is true in Rome, where we witness the work of the Missionaries of Charity of Mother Teresa in the slums. It is also true in Mexico, Paraguay, and Brazil, where the poor are being recognized as the prophets, calling us to simplify our lifestyles. And in the United States, the Catholic Worker and Sojourner's Communities are opening their hearts and their doors to welcome disadvantaged people who become their teachers and their mentors.

Wherever Churches are renewing themselves they are, at the same time, embracing voluntary poverty as the spontaneous response to the evolving movements in the world. Individually and collectively, we want to express criticism of the growing wealth of the few, and our deep solidarity with the growing misery of the many.

What this poverty means concretely in the life of each individual is hard to say, because discernment is needed. We can easily tip over on the side of being too wealthy or on the side of unwise divestment. But I dare to say that anyone who practices contemplative prayer in a disciplined way will be confronted sooner or later with Christ's word to the rich young man. If one thing is certain it is that each of us resembles this rich young person who eventually asks the question: "Teacher, what must I do to possess everlasting life?" What isn't so clear is whether or not we are ready to hear the answer and to act! Like the rich young man, we cling to our secure and comfortable lifestyle. And we also experience sadness.

I am deeply convinced that contemplative prayer and voluntary poverty are the two main pillars supporting those trying to practice celibacy.

CONCLUSION

Trying to summarize and conclude these thoughts on celibacy, I am painfully aware that many of your questions about celibacy have not been addressed at all. I am aware that I have not touched upon the integration of our sexuality with its passions, desires, and needs, and our daily living in a stressful environment. Nor have I touched on the critical impact of the practice of celibacy on community life. I have omitted an exposition of the fruitfulness, the gift, and the joy that accompany celibacy.

I wanted very consciously to avoid emphasizing the usefulness of celibacy. By speaking about celibacy simply as a way of life that makes us more available to others and encourages us to generously share our gifts, or to make ourselves ready to move freely to those in most need, I fear to make celibacy too useful and too narrow. I fear that we will not be conscious enough of the foolishness of making oneself a eunuch for the Kingdom of Heaven (Mt. 19:12).

Jesus never presented celibacy as a very practical, useful, or efficient lifestyle. About celibacy he said, "Let anyone accept this who can." He calls us to be clear that celibacy will never be the most acceptable, understandable, or obvious choice of most people. So for us to make celibacy useful would be more a tribute to the spirit of American pragmatism than a tribute to the spirit of the Gospel.

For us to protect and nurture vacancy for our God in the midst of a society that offers self-fulfillment as our ultimate goal is hardly useful or practical. So let us not be deceived. There is a strong force at work in our world wanting to seduce us. It calls us to believe that standing empty-handed waiting for the Lord is never useful, divesting ourselves of rightful possessions is never practical, and living without an intimate relationship with a companion and without children is certainly never very smart.

But still, contemplative prayer, voluntary poverty, and sexual abstinence are three elements of our celibacy that witness to the beauty of the inner vacancy where we encounter Love, listen to the voice of Love, and celebrate the presence of Love in our midst. When we finally accept the uselessness, impracticality, and foolishness of all this, celibacy proves its effectiveness after all. It is effectiveness that belongs not in our world, but is experienced more in the realm of the Kingdom in our midst. Only those of us who have fully experienced the pain of our emptiness know this effectiveness.

In the circus of life we indeed are the clowns! Let those of us who can do so give ourselves to this incredible calling with all our passion and energy, so that those who meet us will smile as they recognize in us the presence of the One who loves stubborn and hard-headed children with an infinite tenderness and care.

CHAPTER THREE

PRAYER AND THOUGHT

INTRODUCTION

When we think about prayer, we usually regard it as one of the many things we are supposed to do to live a full and mature Christian life. We say to ourselves or to each other, "Don't forget to pray, because prayer is important and without it our lives will be shallow. We need to give our time not only to people, but to God as well!" When we are especially motivated in our conviction that prayer is important, we might even be willing to give a whole hour to prayer every day, or a whole day every month, or a whole week every year. And because of all this, prayer becomes a part, and even a very important part of our lives.

But when the apostle Paul speaks about prayer, he uses a very different language. He does not speak about prayer as a part of life, but as all of life. He does not mention prayer as something we should not forget, but rather he claims it is our ongoing concern. He does not exhort his readers to pray once in a while, regularly, or often, but without shame he admonishes them to pray constantly, unceasingly, and without interruption. Paul does not ask us to spend some of every day in prayer. No, Paul is much more radical. He asks us to pray day and night, in joy and in sorrow, at work and at play, without intermissions or breaks. For Paul, praying is like breathing. It cannot be interrupted without mortal danger.

To the Christians in Thessalonica Paul writes: "Pray constantly, and for all things give thanks to God, because this is what God expects you to do in Christ Jesus" (1 Th. 5:17–18). Paul not only demands unceasing prayer but also he practices it. "We constantly thank God for you" (1 Th. 2:13), he says to his community in Greece. "We feel we must be continually thanking God for you" (2 Th. 1:3). "We pray continually that our God will make you worthy of his call" (2 Th. 1:11). To the Romans he writes: "I never fail to mention you in my prayers" (Rm. 1:9).

*He also comforts his friend Timothy with the words: "Always I
remember you in my prayers" (2 Tm. 1:3).*

The two Greek terms that appear repeatedly in Paul's
letters are *pantote* (always) and *adialeiptos* (without interruption). These words make it clear that for Paul, prayer is not
just a part of living, but all of living; not only a part of his
thought, but all of his thought; not a part of his emotions
and feelings, but all of them. Paul's passion allows no room
for partial commitments, piecemeal caring, or hesitant generosity. He gives all and asks all.

This radical approach to life obviously raises some difficult questions. What is he talking about? What does he
mean by "To pray without ceasing"? How can we possibly
live our already demanding and stressful lives as uninterrupted prayer? What does one do about the endless dis-
tractions that constantly intrude on us? Moreover, how are
we expected to pray when we are asleep or taking some
needed moments of diversion? Can these few hours we use
to escape from the tensions and conflicts of life be lifted up
into some kind of prayer? These questions are real, and
have puzzled many of us on our spiritual journey because
we really wanted to take seriously Paul's exhortation to
"pray without ceasing."

One of the best known examples of the desire for continuous prayer is the story of the nineteenth-century Russian peasant who wanted so much to be obedient to Paul's

call for uninterrupted prayer that he went to the desert to find a *staretz*, a holy person dedicated to an austere life of prayer and sacrifice. He counseled with one, then with another and another, looking for an answer. Finally he found a holy man who taught him the Jesus Prayer. The holy man told the peasant to say thousands of times each day, "Lord Jesus Christ, have mercy on me." The peasant found that by doing this, the Jesus Prayer slowly became united with his breathing and heartbeat. He then traveled through Russia carrying his knapsack with the Bible, the *Philokalia*, and some bread and salt, living a life of unceasing prayer.* Although we are not nineteenth-century Russian peasants with a similar wanderlust, we still share the question of this simple peasant: "How do we pray without ceasing?"

I would like to respond to this question not in the context of the wide, silent Russian steppes of the nineteenth century, but in the context of the restlessness of our contemporary Western society. I want to deepen the call to see unceasing prayer as the conversion of our unceasing thought processes. My central question, therefore, is "How can we turn our perpetual mental activities into perpetual prayer?" or, to express it more simply, "How can thinking become praying?"

First I will invite you to ponder how our unceasing

*See *The Way of the Pilgrim*, translated from the Russian by R. M. French (New York: Seabury Press, 1965).

thinking is a source of our joy as well as of our pain. Then I want you to recognize how this unceasing thinking has the potential to be turned into an uninterrupted conversation with God. Finally I will ask to explore how to develop a discipline that will promote this ongoing conversion from thought to conversation with God. In this way, I hope that unceasing communion with God in prayer can be removed from the sphere of romantic sentimentalism and become a realistic possibility for our demanding lives in a demanding world.

UNCEASING THOUGHTS
Thinking reeds

Lately I have been wondering if we ever do *not* think. It seems to me that we are always involved in some kind of thought process and that being without thoughts is not a real human option. When Blaise Pascal calls a human being a *roseau pensant* (thinking reed), he is trying to explain how our ability to think constitutes our humanity and sets us apart from all other created beings. All our emotions, passions, and feelings are intimately connected with our thoughts so that we can safely say that our thoughts form the cradle in which our joys as well as our sorrows are born. The words *thoughts* and *thinking* are used here in a very broad sense and include different mental processes. When we look at these processes it appears that whether we like it or not, we are involved in, or subjected to, unceasing thoughts.

One of the forms of thinking with which we are most familiar, but which represents only a small part of our mental processes, is reflective thinking. Reflection is a conscious bending back over events and the ideas, images, and emotions connected with these events. It requires the application of our willpower in a concentrated effort; it calls for discipline, endurance, patience, and much mental energy. Those who study a great deal know how hard systematic reflection is and how it can wear us down and even exhaust us. Reflection is real work and does not come easily.

But not reflecting does not mean not thinking. We quite often find ourselves thinking without even realizing that that is what we are doing.

You might be walking through the streets of Rome and find yourself thinking about your hometown, your parents, your brothers and sisters, and then you realize that you had not planned to think about them at all. Or you might suddenly discover that you are thinking about pasta and wine, or about having a lot of money to give away, or about sex, or about what you would say if the President of the United States gave you a phone call. In Rome you might be wondering what name you would choose if they elected you Pope, or what you would say or not

*say about your faith if you were tortured with electric shock, or
about who would cry if you jumped from the fifth floor of the
American College. You might be dreaming about how you would
act if you happened to be married or ordained or a parent . . . and
on and on. You never planned to think about these things nor had
you even wanted to think about them, but you catch your mind in
midstream and realize that you are moving into a complex network of ideas, images, and feelings.*

This passive, prereflective thinking is sometimes disturbing, and we wonder where it comes from. Occasionally
it makes us anxious or apprehensive. We realize that our
mind thinks things that we cannot control, things that
sneak up on us, coming from nowhere to interfere with our
best intentions. During the most solemn moments we may
find ourselves thinking the most banal thoughts. While listening to a sermon about God's love, we find ourselves
wondering about the haircut of the preacher. While reading a spiritual book, we suddenly realize that our mind is
busy with the questions about what's for dinner or the letters we haven't written or the painful telephone call that
must be made. While watching a beautiful ceremony at
Church we notice ourselves trying to figure out how to
relate with teenage sons and daughters, to ask for a raise at
work, or to reduce the tension between ourselves and our
spouses. Indeed, not infrequently we catch ourselves thinking very low things during very high moments. The prob-

lem, however, is that we cannot think about nothing. We have to think, and we often feel betrayed by our own uncontrolled or uncontrollable thoughts.

Our thought processes, by reaching even into our sleeping hours, go even deeper than our reflective moments and our uncontrolled mental wanderings. We might wake up in the middle of the night and find ourselves part of a frightening car race, a delicious banquet, or a heavenly choir. Sometimes we are able to give a detailed account of all the things that happened to us in our dreams: what we heard as well as what we said. Sometimes we remember only the final moment of our dream, and sometimes we are left with only a vague fear or an undefined joy. We know that much is going on during our sleep, of which, only occasionally, we catch bits and pieces. Careful brain-wave studies show that our minds are always active during sleep; we are always dreaming even when we have no recollection of our dream or their content. And, although we tend to regard our dream processes as insignificant in comparison with our daytime reflections or our undirected mental wanderings, we should not forget that for many people dreams prove to be the main source of knowing. Remember the patriarch Jacob who heard God's call when he saw the angels going up and down a ladder? Also, in the Old Testament Joseph was banished to Egypt because he irritated his brothers with his visions of sheaves, sun, moon, and stars bowing to him. And in the New Testament

Joseph fled to Egypt with Mary and the child, after he had seen in his dream, an angel warning him of Herod. In our century, so far from biblical times, we find Sigmund Freud and Carl Jung informing us that our dreams will tell us our truth.

Source of joy and sorrow

I say all this to reiterate how we are indeed involved in unceasing thought day and night, willingly or unwillingly, during our most alert moments and during our deepest sleep, while working and while resting. This is our human predicament, a predicament that causes us great joy and immense pain. Our ceaseless thought is our burden as well as our gift, and sometimes we might wish to be able to stop thinking for a while. Perhaps if that were possible we would not be haunted by the memory of lost friends, or the awareness of past breakages with those we love, or by our knowledge and sense of helplessness when confronted by hunger and oppression in our world. These thoughts impose themselves on us at the most unwelcome hours, and they can keep us awake when we are most in need of sleep. We yearn to be free of ceaseless thinking so as to erase the disturbing graffiti etched on our minds. But there is another side. Without thought there would be no smile, no laughter, no quiet joy. How could we be glad to see friends again when we are unable to think of them? How could we celebrate a birthday, a national holiday, or a great religious feast if our minds were not aware of the meaning of the event? How could we be grateful if we couldn't remember the gifts we have received? How would it be possible to lift up our hearts and sing and dance without the connections that our thoughts are constantly making for us?

Our thoughts form the cradle where sorrow and joy are held. With an empty mind our hearts would not mourn or feast, our eyes would not cry or laugh, our hands would not wring or clap, our tongues would not curse or praise. Thus, as "thinking reeds," we are also enabled to feel deeply and experience life to the full with all its many sorrows and joys. All that remains is that this unceasing activity at the core of our minds and beings must gradually be transformed, slowly, slowly, but persistently, into unceasing communion with God.

UNCEASING PRAYER
In dialogue

To pray unceasingly, as Paul asks us to do, would be completely impossible if it meant to think constantly about God, not only for people who have many different concerns to occupy their minds but also for monks who spend many hours a day in prayer. Thinking about God all the time is an unrealistic expectation that might cause mental imbalance.

To be continually in communion with God does not mean thinking about God in contrast to thinking about other things, nor does it mean spending time with God instead of spending time with other people. As soon as we begin to divide off our thoughts into thoughts about God and thoughts about other things like people and events, we separate God from our daily life. At that point God is allocated to a pious little niche in some corner of our lives where we only think pious thoughts and experience pious feelings. Although it is important and even indispensable for our spiritual lives to set apart time for God and God alone, our prayer can only become unceasing communion when all our thoughts—beautiful or ugly, high or low, proud or shameful, sorrowful or joyful—can be thought in the presence of the One who dwells in us and surrounds us. By trying to do this, our unceasing thinking is converted into unceasing prayer moving us from a self-centered monologue to a God-centered dialogue. To do this we want to try to convert our thoughts into conversation. The main question, therefore, is not so much what we think, but to whom we present our thoughts, because to pray unceasingly means to think and live in the *presence* of Love.

It is not hard to see how real a change takes place in our daily life when we find the courage to keep our thoughts to ourselves no longer, but to speak out, confess them, share them, bring them into conversation. As soon as an embarrassing or exhilarating idea is taken out of its isolation and brought into a relationship with

*someone, something totally new happens. Doing so obviously
requires much courage and trust, precisely because we are not
always sure how our thoughts will be received. But as soon as we
have taken the risk and experience acceptance, our thoughts themselves receive a new quality.*

To pray unceasingly is to channel our thoughts out of
their fearful isolation into a fearless conversation with God.
Jesus' life was a life lived in the presence of the Father,
whom he loved. Jesus kept nothing, absolutely nothing,
hidden from his Father. Jesus' joys, his fears, his hopes, and
his despairs were always shared in communion with his
Father. Therefore, Jesus could indeed say to his disciples:
". . . you will be scattered . . . leaving me alone. And yet I
am not alone, because the Father is with me" (Jn. 16:32).
Thus prayer asks us to break out of our monologue with
ourselves and to imitate Jesus by turning our lives into an
unceasing conversation with the One we call God.

Prayer, therefore, is not introspection. Introspection
means to look inward, to enter into the complex network
of our mental processes in search of some inner logic or
some elucidating connections. Introspection results from
the desire to know ourselves better and to become more
familiar with our own interiority. Although introspection
has a positive role in our thought processes, there is a danger that it may entangle us in a labyrinth of our own ideas,
feelings, and emotions and lead us to an increasing self-

preoccupation. Introspection often causes paralyzing worries or unproductive self-gratification. Introspection has the potential to create moodiness, and this moodiness is a very widespread phenomenon in our society. It betrays our great concern with ourselves and our undue sensitivity to all our thoughts and feelings. It leads us to experience life as a constant fluctuation between "feeling high" and "feeling low," between "good days" and "bad days," and thus becomes a form of narcissism.

Prayer is not introspection. It is not a scrupulous, inward-looking analysis of our own thoughts and feelings but it is an attentiveness to the Presence of Love personified inviting us to an encounter. Prayer is the presentation of our thoughts—reflective, as well as daydreams, and night dreams—to the One who receives them, sees them in the light of unconditional love, and responds to them with divine compassion. This context of thinking in the Presence, of conversation and dialogue with Love is the joyful affirmation of our gentle Companion on the journey with God who knows our minds and hearts, our goodness and our beauty, our darkness and our light. The Psalmist prays the prayer for us in Psalm 139:

O Lord, you search me and you know me,
you know my resting and my rising,
you discern my purpose from afar.
You mark when I walk or lie down,

all my ways lie open to you [1–3]
O search me, God, and know my heart.
O test me and know my thoughts.
See that I follow not the wrong path
*and lead me in the path of life eternal [23–24].**

The movement from thinking random thoughts to living in communion with Love is a radical conversion of our mental processes. Gradually we move away from ourselves —our worries, preoccupations, and self-gratifications— and we direct all that we recognize as ours to the One who loves us, trusting that through love all will be made new.

Unexpected idolatries

But this conversion from unceasing thought to unceasing prayer is very slow and far from easy. There is a deep resistance to allowing ourselves to become so vulnerable, so naked, and so totally unprotected. There is no question about our desire to love God. We want to be men and women who love and worship God, but we also want to protect a little corner of our inner lives for ourselves. We cling to a protected space where we might sometimes hide out with our own secret thoughts, our dreams and fantasies, and our play with our own mental fabrications. When we begin to think about living and thinking always in God's

*Grail translation, Paulist Press.

loving presence we experience the immediate temptation to select carefully the thoughts that we bring into our conversations with God and the ones we reserve for our own private time.

What makes us so frightened and stingy? Maybe we wonder if God can handle all that goes on in our minds and hearts. Is God up to accepting our hateful thoughts, our cruel fantasies, and our shameful dreams? Can our compassionate Brother handle our primitive images, our inflated illusions, and our exotic mental castles? Or do we want to hold onto our own pleasurable imaginings and stimulating reveries, afraid that in showing them to our Lord, we may have to give them up? We shuffle forward and backward, desiring intimate communion and seduced to selfish introspection. Fear mixes with our yearnings and greed with our generosity, and we gradually become aware of how much those secret meanderings are most in need of Love's healing touch.

This withholding from God of a large part of our thoughts leads us onto a road that we probably would never consciously want to take. It is the road of idolatry. Idolatry means the worship of false images, and that is precisely what happens when we keep our fantasies, worries, and joys to ourselves and do not present them to the Lord of our hearts. By refusing to share these thoughts, we limit our own healing, erecting little altars to the mental images we are withholding from the divine conversation.

I vividly remember how I once visited a psychiatrist to complain about my difficulty in controlling my fantasy life. I told him that disturbing images kept coming up and that I found it hard to detach myself from them. When he had listened to my story, he smiled and said, "Well, Father, as a priest you should know that this is idolatry, because your God is saying that you should not worship false images." Only then did I realize fully what it really means to confess having sinned not only in word and action but also in thought. It means confessing idolatry, one of the oldest and most pervasive temptations.

So let me reiterate how unceasing communion is not immediately available to us, precisely because we like to hold onto certain aspects of our inner life for ourselves alone. This experience of resistance to generously entrusting ourselves to Love personified is very real and very ingrained. Unceasing prayer is a true, bitter, and ongoing struggle against idolatry. When all our thoughts—those of our days as well as those of our nights—have been brought into a loving conversation with God, then we know obedience in its fullness. And since this is obviously a task that is never fully completed, we need to raise another question: the question of discipline. I realize that *discipline* is not a very popular word, but it comes from the word *disciple*, and somehow we must try to view it with new eyes. So we ask, What disciplines or practices help us to become followers and disciples of Love? What must we do to give ourselves totally into the hands of our Way, our Truth, and our Life?

DISCIPLINES
Imagining Christ

Because of the many resistances to the conversion of our unceasing thought into unceasing communion, we need support. This is where "disciplines" come to the rescue. Without the help of certain disciplines, unceasing prayer remains a vague ideal, something that has perhaps a romantic appeal but something that is not at all realistic in our contemporary world. Discipline implies that something very specific and concrete will need to be chosen to create a context or an environment in which a life of uninterrupted prayer is nurtured. Unceasing prayer is deeply nourished by the discipline of committed time for solitude and prayer. Setting aside a certain place and time each day to do nothing else but pray creates the context for unceasing thought to become unceasing prayer. Why is this planned prayer-practice so important? It is important because by dedicating ourselves to a specific time and place for nothing but our openness to God's presence, we focus and wait in hope to welcome God's Spirit as our partner in a dialogue of life and love.

This discipline of prayer embraces different ways of praying: communally and individually, as well as orally and silently. It is of primary importance that we enter our daily solitude with an understanding of its potential and with hope and expectation of being with God. We often say, "All of life should be lived in gratitude," but this gratitude is only possible if at certain times we give thanks in a very concrete and visible way. We often say, "All our days should be lived for the glory of God," but this is only possible if a day is regularly set apart to give glory to God. We often say, "We should love one another always," but this is only possible if we regularly perform generous and unambiguous acts of love. Similarly, it is true that we can only say, "All our thoughts should be conversation and communion with God," if there are times when we stop and allow God to be our only occupation and thought.

Beneath all our prayer, whether it be the celebrations in Church, or contemplative, is our effort to be open and attentive to the God we know from Scripture and experience. With this in mind, I would like to share in greater detail the importance and the implications of the discipline of what is known as contemplation. Contemplation is one of the sure roads to unceasing communion with the Beloved. Although many good things have been written about contemplation and contemplative prayer, most of us still hold onto the impression that contemplative prayer is something other-worldly, very special, very "high," or very difficult, and really not for ordinary people like us with ordinary jobs and ordinary problems. This is sad and unfortunate, because the practice, or the discipline, of contemplative prayer is particularly precious and life-giving precisely for busy people like us who are so busy and fragmented. If it is true that each of us is called to the conversion of our thoughts into an ongoing conversation with our Lord, then contemplative prayer can be a discipline that puts us into position for radical transformation.

Contemplative prayer is truly quite simple and wonderful. Contemplation is about looking and waiting for God. It is about gazing at Jesus and at the Father. "How is this possible," you might ask, "since nobody has ever seen God?"

We know that Jesus was sent by God into the world. This mystery, called the Incarnation, makes it possible for us to see the living God in and through Jesus Christ. Jesus is the Beloved Son of God. Jesus is God-in-the-flesh. In and through the life of Jesus, we are introduced to God as the loving Father of Jesus. By looking at and listening to Jesus, and by following him through the pages of Scripture, we are looking at, listening to, and following the One who is the image of God.

Jesus is the Son of the living God. When Jesus spoke to the disciples about God, Philip said impatiently, "Lord, let us see the Father, and then we shall be satisfied." Jesus answered, "To have seen me is to have seen the Father, so how can you say, 'Let us see the Father'? Do you not believe that I am in the Father and the Father is in me?" (Jn. 14:10).

Contemplative prayer, therefore, is to see Jesus Christ as the image of God. In contemplative prayer all our images of our God, conscious or unconscious will be shaped and formed by God's Son, our living example, the only image of God. This is contemplation.

Contemplative prayer can be described as an imagining of God's Son, Jesus, a letting him enter fully into our consciousness so that he becomes the icon always present in the inner room of our hearts. By gazing at Jesus, walking on the earth, we give him loving attention and we "see" with our minds and hearts how he is the way to the Father. Jesus' life and work is an uninterrupted union with and contemplation of his Father. We, as followers of Jesus, try to enter into the same disposition. We welcome the discipline of contemplation, taking time regularly to enter into the life of Jesus to contemplate the incredible bond between Jesus and the Father. And we trust that in, through, and with Jesus, we too may live and bask in God's unconditional love.

A simple example

Practically, how do we contemplate Jesus? How do we enter into dialogue with him and allow our unceasing thought to be transformed into unceasing prayer? There is no single answer to this question, because each one of us is invited to develop a personal discipline of spending time with God, according to our particular life and work, our daily schedule, cultural heritage, and personality. The wonderful thing about discipline is how by its nature it will conform to the particular lifestyle of the individual who is seeking God. Discipline supports us in our desire to follow Jesus and experience communion with our beloved Father. So, rather than give a further description of contemplative prayer, I will try to offer you one example of a contemplative prayer discipline. I do this in the hope that it might open some doors for you to try to discover your particular way of fidelity to a life where contemplation is central.

One very simple discipline is to read, every evening before going to sleep, the readings of the next day's Eucharistic service with special attention to the Gospel. Be attentive to anything that touches you. You may find it helpful to take one sentence or word that corresponds to your experience or which offers you special comfort. Repeat the word or sentence a few times and let that one sentence or word open your heart to the whole content of the story or the message. Repeat the sentence or word and let the content slowly descend from your mind into your heart and center.

Personally, I have found this practice to be a powerful support in times of crisis. It is especially helpful during the night, when worries or anxieties keep me awake and seduce me into idolatry. By remembering the Gospel story or the saying of an Old or New Testament author, I enter into another realm, a safe, inner home where I am not alone with all my preoccupations. They are with me, but they are somehow transformed into quiet prayer. The Gospel story leads me to the inner sanctum.

During the following day, schedule a specific time for solitude and contemplation. It could be previously marked in your agenda planner. This is your commitment to look at Jesus as he appears in the reading. You do this by slowly rereading the Gospel of the day. Put yourself in the picture and try to imagine the Lord as he speaks or acts before you and the people. During this time-set-apart you look at Jesus, listen to him, touch him, and let him become present in your whole being.

In contemplative prayer we meet Jesus, our healer, our teacher, and our guide. We are present with him in his indignation, in his compassion, in his suffering, and in his glory. We walk with him, look at him, listen to him, and enter into conversation with him. Often the other readings of the day from the Old and New Testament intensify our experience and our image of Jesus. Vincent van Gogh once remarked that the Gospels are the top of the mountain and the other biblical writings form the slopes.

For me, this discipline of having an "empty time" just to be in communion with Jesus as he speaks to me, in the readings of the day, has proven very powerful. I have discovered that during the rest of the day, wherever I am or whatever I am doing, the image of Christ that I have contemplated during that "empty time" is in me as a beautiful icon. Sometimes it is the conscious center of my thoughts, but more often it is a quiet presence of which I am only indirectly aware. In the beginning I hardly noticed the difference. Slowly, however, I realized that I carry Jesus, the image of God, inside of me, and he works in me to transform my reflective thoughts as well as my frenzied ones and my daydreams. I am truly convinced that this simple form of daily contemplation is very gradually converting my dreams into the gateway of God's ongoing, ever-loving, presence and revelation.

Finally, this discipline of taking into ourselves Jesus as revealed in the Gospel puts the celebration of daily Eucharist into a totally new perspective. Especially when it is celebrated in the evening, the Eucharist becomes a real climax in which the Lord with whom we have journeyed during the day meets us again and now speaks to us again as a community of believers. In the Eucharist, Jesus invites us with our friends to come and be with him around the table. It is a moment of incredible intimacy, and it is there that the transformation of all our images into his image finds its fullest realization. It is there at the "table of the Lord" that our communion with Jesus, experienced in contemplation, finds its perfection. Daily contemplation prepares us for the daily transforming celebration of Eucharist. Because we are working on the practice of living the whole day in the presence of Love, the Eucharist ceases to be merely a routine or an obligation. It becomes instead the center of daily life, the moment of intimate communion with the Beloved.

One of my most joyful discoveries was how the experience of daily contemplative prayer uncovered for me the transforming power of the daily celebration of the Eucharist. The Eucharist becomes for me a deep experience of intimacy, a special moment and a special place from which I draw light, strength, and hope. I have come to realize that our most private times of contemplation are not only good for us individually but are also, in the final analysis, a service to the whole community.

This simple discipline of prayer becomes a strong, supportive structure where our unceasing thought becomes unceasing communion with the Lord. In our contemplative prayer, Jesus is no longer a stranger who lived long ago in a foreign world. Rather, Jesus is for us a living presence to whom we can relate. We are in dialogue with the living God, here and now.

The contemplative practice I have described is only one of many possible examples. I offer it merely as a suggestion that points in the direction of a disciplined prayer life. The important thing is that we realize the beautiful Christian ideal of making our whole life into a prayer remains nothing but an ideal unless we are willing to work at it. If we choose certain supportive disciplines they lead us into the realm of great possibilities. We are choosing to do something to realize our deep desire for real intimacy and communion. Faithful to our daily practice, we gradually enter more and more consciously and explicitly into an encounter with Love Itself.

CONCLUSION

I have tried to show that unceasing prayer is not the unusual feat of a simple Russian peasant but a realistic vocation for each one of us. It certainly is not a way of living that comes either automatically by our simply desiring it or easily by our just praying once in a while. But when we give it serious attention and develop an appropriate discipline, we experience real transformation in our lives that leads us closer and closer to God. Total communion with God as a permanent and unchangeable state of mind obviously will never be attained. We can only follow our desire and give it attention and discipline. In doing this we gradually become aware that many of the disturbing thoughts that seemed to distract us are being transformed into the ongoing praise of God. And as we begin to know God with increasing clarity and to appreciate God's beauty, we also recognize how we are less distracted by people and things. On the contrary, God's creation speaks to us in many ways about the One we contemplate. We slowly become conscious of the truth about our prayer that is neither more nor less than the constant practice of the presence of God at all times and in all places.

Paul's words to the Christians of Thessalonica about unceasing prayer might at first have seemed demanding and unrealistic. And at first sight they are! But I hope we now see that they are also a source of ever-increasing joy.

After all, it is not just Paul, but also the divine Lover who invites us to let our whole life be transformed. That is why Paul could write: "Pray constantly, and for all things give thanks to God, because this is what God expects you to do in Christ Jesus" (1 Th. 5:17).

CHAPTER FOUR

CONTEMPLATION AND CARING

INTRODUCTION

One epithet Rome certainly deserves is City of Statues. You cannot walk for long in the streets of Rome without encountering marble characters, some playful, others fierce; some beautiful, others ugly; some sensual, others spiritual. On one of my walks I met the little stone elephant with an Egyptian obelisk on his back. Looking at this friendly animal, I was reminded of a short story.

There was once a sculptor working hard with his hammer and chisel on a large block of marble. A little boy who was watching him saw nothing more than large and small pieces of stone falling away left and right. He had no idea what was happening. But when the boy returned to the studio a few weeks later, he saw to his great surprise a large, powerful lion sitting in the place where the marble had stood. With great excitement the boy ran to the sculptor and said, "Sir, tell me, how did you know there was a lion in the marble?"*

The art of sculpture is, first of all, the art of seeing. In one block of marble, Michelangelo saw a loving mother holding her dead son on her lap, while in another, he saw a self-confident David ready to hurl his stone at the approaching Goliath, and in a third, he saw an irate Moses at the point of rising in anger from his seat. Visual art is indeed the art of seeing, and the practice of disciplines is a way to make visible what has been seen. The skillful artist is a liberator who frees from bondage the figures hidden for billions of years inside the marble. The artist reveals the true identity of the figures!

The image of the sculptor offers us a beautiful illustration of the relationship between contemplation and caring or ministry. To contemplate is to *see*, and to minister is to *make visible*; the contemplative life is a life with a vision, and the life of caring for others is a life revealing the vision to others.

*This story was inspired by Thomas Hora's *Existential Metapsychiatry* (New York: Seabury Press, 1977), p. 20.

I arrived at this definition through the writings of Evagrius Ponticus, one of the Desert Fathers who had great influence on monastic spirituality in the East and the West. Evagrius calls contemplation a *theoria physike*, which means a vision (*theoria*) of the nature of things (*physike*). The contemplative is someone who sees things for what they really are, who sees the real connections, who knows—as Thomas Merton used to say—"what the scoop is." As I said before, to see the vision we choose the practice of certain disciplines.

Evagrius calls discipline the *praktike*; removing the blindfolds that prevent us from seeing clearly. Merton, himself very familiar with the writings of Evagrius, expressed the same idea. He told the monks at Gethsemani Abbey that the contemplative life is a life in which we constantly move from opaqueness to transparency, from the place where things are dark, impenetrable, and closed, to the place where these same things are translucent, open, and offer vision far beyond themselves. He says it so well!

In this reflection, I will look first at the different levels where this movement from opaqueness to transparency occurs, because that makes it clear to us how our lives become a *theoria physike*, a vision of the very nature of things. Then I will explore the *praktike*, the concrete discipline of communion with God in contemplation that must undergird the living passage from opaqueness to transparency. In so doing I hope we will understand more clearly the relationship between being and doing, between contemplation and ministry. This relationship is as intimate as the relationship between the vision and the discipline of the sculptor.

CONTEMPLATIVE LIFE

Contemplative life, as Evagrius describes it, is a life that leads us to see our world as a transparent world, a world that points beyond itself. Finding God in prayer reveals the true nature of our world to us. Just as a window cannot be a real window for us if we cannot look through it, so our world cannot show to us its real identity if it remains opaque and does not point beyond itself. You and I, on a seeking journey, must therefore try to move continuously from opaqueness to transparency in three central relationships: our relationship with nature, with time, and with people.

Nature

In recent decades we have become particularly aware of the crucial importance of our relationship with nature. As long as we relate to the trees, the rivers, the mountains, the fields, and the oceans as our properties to be manipulated by us according to our real or fabricated needs, nature remains opaque and does not reveal to us its true being. When we relate to a tree as nothing more than a potential chair, it cannot speak much to us about growth. When a river is only a dumping place for our industrial wastes, it no longer informs us about movement. And when we relate to a flower as nothing more than a model for a plastic decoration, the flower loses its power to reveal to us the simple beauty of life. When we relate to nature primarily as property to be used, it becomes opaque, and this opaqueness is manifest in our society as pollution. The dirty rivers, the smog-filled skies, the strip-mined hills, and the ravaged woods are sad signs of our false relationship with nature.

Our difficult and very urgent task is to accept the truth that nature is not primarily a property to be possessed, but a gift to be received with admiration and gratitude. Only when we make a deep bow to the rivers, oceans, hills, and mountains that offer us a home, only then can they become transparent and reveal to us their real meaning.

A friend once gave me a beautiful photograph of a water lily. I asked him how he had been able to take such a splendid picture. With a smile he said, "Well, I had to be very patient and very attentive. It was only after a few hours of compliments that the lily was willing to let me take her picture."

All nature conceals its deepest secret and cannot reveal its hidden wisdom and profound beauty if we do not listen carefully and patiently. John Henry Newman sees nature as a veil through which an invisible world is intimated. He writes: "The visible world is . . . the veil of the world invisible . . . so that all that exists or happens visibly, conceals and yet suggests, and above all subserves, a system of persons, facts and events beyond itself."*

How differently we would live if we were constantly aware of this veil and sensed in our whole being how nature is ever ready for us to hear and see the great story of the Creator's love, to which it points. The plants and animals with whom we live teach us about birth, growth, maturation, and death, about the need for gentle care, and especially about the importance of patience and hope. And even more profoundly, water, oil, bread, and wine all point beyond themselves to the great story of our re-creation.

It is sad that in our days we are less connected with nature and we no longer allow nature to minister to us. We so easily limit ministry to work for people by people. But we could do an immense service to our world if we would let nature heal, counsel, and teach again.

I often wonder if the sheer artificiality and ugliness with which many people are surrounded are not as bad or worse than their interpersonal problems.

*Essays Critical and Historical, Vol. II (London: Longmans, Green, and Co., 1901), p. 192.

I have found this painfully true in trying to care for the elderly. Old people suffer from the ugliness of their environment and I trust that much healing and peace are available to older people if only we help them make their homes or rooms a little more beautiful. With real plants that grow and die as they do and ask for care and attention as they do, the lives of the elderly might be less lonely. There is more going on between plants and people than we realize. Perhaps real flowers, about which and to which we can speak, have more healing power than well-chosen words about the meaning of life and death.

Those who are sensitive to the enormous ecological problem of our age and work hard to take away some of nature's opaqueness are doing real ministry for us and for our universe. They are wise enough to allow not only people but also plants and animals to speak about the cycle of life, to heal the lonely, and to tell of the great love of the Lord. Let us endeavor to make the passage from opaqueness to transparency in our relationship with nature. Transparency not only leads us to a deeper knowledge and vision of the world, but it also contributes generously to our lives of teaching, healing, and worship.

Time

A second relationship in which the contemplative life calls us to the ongoing movement from opaqueness to transparency is our relationship with time. Time constantly threatens to become our great enemy. In our contemporary society it often seems that not money but time enslaves us. We say, "I wish I could do all the things that I need to do, but I simply have no time. Just thinking about all the things I have to do today—writing five letters, visiting a friend, practicing my music, making a phone call, shopping, cooking, and cleaning—just thinking about these things makes me tired." Indeed, it seems that we often feel we no longer have time, because time has us! We sometimes experience ourselves as victims of an ongoing pressure to meet deadlines, to do our tasks within short time periods, and to be ready on time. In simple conversation we frequently hear the excuse, "I am sorry, but I have no time." And when we approach each other for support or favors we preface our request with "I know how busy you are, but do you have just a minute?" We hasten over a quick lunch or "while grabbing a bite" to make important decisions. A strange sense of always being in a hurry pervades our consciousness as we watch the time in front of us filling up so quickly. It causes us to sometimes wonder, "Who or what is pushing me? Why am I so busy that I have no time left to live?"

All this suggests how time has become opaque, dark, and impenetrable, and we experience it as *chronos*. Life is nothing more than a chronology, a randomly collected series of incidents and accidents over which we have no control. To experience life in this way soon leads us to depression and a sense of fatalism, and the fatalism sometimes manifests itself under the guise of boredom. Boredom does not mean that we have nothing to do but we are gnawed by the feeling that whatever we do or say makes no real difference. Boredom is the feeling that the real decisions are made somewhere apart from us, independent of our words or actions.

Boredom, therefore, is a symptom of living in time as *chronos*. The paradox of *chronos* is that we are most subject to boredom precisely when we are in a hurry, overly busy, or rushing to meet deadlines. This boredom reveals how opaque time has become for us.

When we choose to spend quality time daily with the Lord, we become slowly aware that time loses its opaqueness and becomes transparent. This is often a very difficult and slow passage, but it is full of re-creating power. To start seeing that the many events of our day, week, or year are not in the way of our search for a full life but are rather the way to it is a real experience of conversion. We discover that cleaning and cooking, writing letters and doing professional work, visiting people and caring for others, are not a series of random events that prevent us from realizing our deepest self. These natural, daily activities contain within themselves some transforming power that changes how we live. We make a hidden passage from time lived as *chronos* to time lived as *kairos*. *Kairos* is a Greek word meaning "the opportunity." It is the right time, the real moment, the chance of our lives. When our time becomes *kairos*, it frees us and opens us to endless new possibilities. Living *kairos* offers us an opportunity for a profound change of heart.

In Jesus' life, every event becomes *kairos*. He opens his public ministry with the words "The time has come" (Mk. 1:15), and he lives every moment of it as an opportunity. Finally, he announces that his time is near (Mk. 26:10) and enters into his last hour as the *kairos*. In so doing he liberates history from its fatalistic chronology.

Jesus' life and death is truly Good News because it reveals to us how all the events of our lives, and even such dark events as war, famine and flood, violence and murder, are not irreversible fatalities. Each moment is like a seed that carries within itself the possibility of becoming *the* moment of change. So what seemed nothing more than flying pieces of marble begins to reveal itself as the important, necessary, and sometimes painful removal of what prevented us from seeing the true image of God. As we live this passage, we no longer feel seduced to run from present time in search of the place where we think life is really happening. We begin to have a truer vision of the world and of our lives in relationship to time and eternity. We begin to glimpse something of eternity in time. At this point boredom falls away and the joyful and painful moments of our lives take on new and profound meaning. It is then that we know that for us time is becoming transparent.

The contemplative life, therefore, is not a life that offers us a few good moments between the many bad ones, but a life that transforms all our time into a window through which the invisible world becomes visible.

The core of all real caring and ministry is to make time transparent so that in the most concrete circumstances of life we see in time the deeper vision of life. Wasting time in communion with the Father in prayer is anything but a waste, because from it we see the hand of God with us each moment and we live each moment as an opportunity of solidarity with God and neighbor. We live time as *kairos*. Those who suffer—the elderly, the poor, and those who are physically, mentally, or spiritually imprisoned—are burdened with a sense of fatalism. But our life of prayer and caring may help to break the chains of this fatalism, and perhaps we can support others on their journey to see the real nature of what they are being asked to live. At this point we claim our discipleship by bringing good news to the poor, new sight to the blind, and liberty to the captives (Lk. 4:18).

People

The third relationship inviting us to move from opaqueness to transparency is our relationship with others. With people, more than in the two previous relationships, the importance of our daily time of solitude and contemplation as *theoria physike*—as seeing the real connections—becomes manifest. We have been conditioned to relate to people as interesting characters or as individuals who strike us as worthy of special attention because of their special qualities. Aren't we always intrigued by interesting characters? Whether they are film stars or criminals, sports heroes or killers, Nobel Prize winners or perverts we are curious about them and about their lives. Sometimes we become fascinated, and we are instinctively drawn to move closer to one or more of these unusual individuals. We want to meet them, shake their hands, get their autographs, or be close enough to gaze at them. The magazine *People* makes millions of dollars catering to human curiosity about famous men and women, while the front pages of our newspapers give less and less actual news and more and more pictures and reports of human irregularities, whether they evoke praise or blame.

> *Rome is wonderful in this way and, remarkably enough, one of the best cities to observe this phenomenon on both sides of the Tiber! Religious journals and secular newspapers create the illusion that not only is the earth dominated by kidnappers and the sky by hijackers, but also that the clerical world around us is richly endowed with curious characters.*

As long as the people we meet and relate to are little more than interesting characters to us, they remain opaque.

No one who is approached as an "interesting character" will reveal to us the inner beauty or the secret of his or her life. On the contrary, characterization is extremely narrowing and limiting and makes all of us close in and hide our real and precious identity. Especially if we are in the field of the helping professions, we tend to quickly and quietly label people with easy characterizations, thus giving us the illusion of understanding. Not only psychiatric labels such as "neurotic," "psychopathic," or "schizophrenic," but also religious labels such as "unbeliever," "pagan," "sinner," "progressive," "conservative," "liberal," and "orthodox" provide a false understanding of the actual person and reveal more about our insecurities than about the real nature of our neighbors.

Fear is a big block, and so we are often afraid in our relationships with each other. We want to try to prevent our fears from putting people into boxes. We want to try to be open to recognize our brothers and our sisters and we want to work hard to give them the dignity and respect they deserve as children of the Father we know.

The word *person* comes from *personare*, which means "sounding through." In our lives we want to "sound through" in our relationships with each other, having enough space within us to recognize and know more than is immediately evident about another. We faithfully try to "sound through" to love greater than we ourselves can grasp, truth deeper than we ourselves can articulate, and beauty richer than we ourselves can imagine. We are called to be transparent to each other and thus to point far beyond our external characteristics to the true Author of love, truth, and beauty.

> *It is possible that when someone says, "I love you," or "I am deeply moved by you," or "I am grateful to you," you immediately become defensive and wonder what is so special about you. You might say or think, "Aren't there many other people who are much more lovable or much more intelligent than I am?" But then you have forgotten that you are a person who sounds through to others something much greater and deeper than you yourself can hear.*

Taking time daily to contemplate the beauty and the mystery of our God as *theoria physike*, as seeing what is really there, has deep and profound significance in our interpersonal relationships. We may not hear or see many visible images of our "sounding through," but we are nevertheless seeing beyond and below the visual impressions we may have of each other. Fear falls away and our real gifts and the gifts of the other are recognizable and known. We are less reticent to affirm each other and to receive from each other in mutuality and care.

Perhaps now we begin to see the intimate connection between contemplation and ministry, between communion with God and caring for each other. Our time of being with God gives us new eyes to see the beauty and gifts in those for whom we care, and our caring is also transformed. We were not expecting to receive from the person in need, but by our reception and affirmation of what we hear "sounding through" them they become gifts for us. And we hope and trust that our recognition of their beauty may support them to come to a recognition and acceptance of their unique and mysterious value.

What more beautiful ministry is there than the ministry through which we help others to become aware of the love, truth, and beauty they reveal to us? Ours is a time in which so many of us doubt our self-worth. We hover on the verge of self-condemnation that takes the very life out of us. So in reaching out to help another, our caring or ministry becomes nurturing and fruitful. We see through the other to the hidden gifts that ask to be shared and we both find new life and energy.

Innumerable people suffer from being unable to give anything. Young people are made to feel that they know little or nothing; adults doubt that they have a real contribution to make; and millions of people in the cities, towns, and villages of this world wonder if they are of any importance to anyone. How beautiful, then, is the ministry through which we call forth and receive the hidden gifts of people. How amazing to celebrate with them the love, truth, and beauty they give to us. This is the nature of prayer and caring. Contemplation enriches ministry and vice versa, filling us with an ever-increasing joy. God is revealed to us in the ever changing lives of people, and the beauty of each brother or sister removes the veil covering the face of God.

There is a continual movement in our contemplation and ministry from opaqueness to transparency. It is the movement from nature as a property to be possessed to nature as a gift to be received with admiration and gratitude. It is the movement from time as a randomly thrown-together series of incidents and accidents to time as a constant opportunity for a change of heart. Finally, it is the movement from people as interesting characters to people sounding through more of themselves than they ever could have believed. This does not mean that nature is never property, that time is never *chronos*, and that people are never interesting characters. It *does* mean that if these were to become the dominant modes of relating to our world, our world would remain opaque and we would never see how things really connect. When, however, we are able slowly to remove our blindfolds and see nature as gift, time as *kairos*, and people as persons, we will also see that our whole world is a sacrament that constantly reveals to us the great love of God. That is the real nature of things—*theoria physike*—about which Evagrius spoke.

CONTEMPLATIVE PRAYER
The lion in the heart

Finally, let us look directly at the practice of contemplative prayer. If we look at the *theoria physike* without also looking at the *praktike*, we are quickly deceived. It is so easy to develop a romantic view of prayer and contemplation and its relationship to ministry. But a contemplative life is the choice of a way of living where all of creation—nature, time, and people—becomes transparent and speaks to us about God and about God's love for us. But this all-embracing view of contemplation might suggest that caring and praying are all the same. This is a large oversimplification. If we say, "My work is my prayer," we forget that the act of seeing requires a well-trained eye.

The little boy's question to the sculptor is a very real question, perhaps the most important question of all: "Sir, tell me, how did you know that there was a lion in the marble?"

How do you and I know that God becomes visible through the veil of nature? How do we come to the realization that all of our time is also an opportunity for a change of heart? How do we know that people sound through more than they themselves can hear? These realities are certainly not obvious, because for most of us the world is very opaque. We recognize nothing in the marble but a thick, impenetrable block of stone. Aren't we romantics, after all, people who are unwilling to see the hard facts of life and who simply see what we want to see?

We are touching here the central questions of our whole lives and of all our praying and caring. Is there a lion in the marble? Is there a loving God, a Presence in this world? Or is this journey of our hearts and spirits to know God through prayer nothing more than wishful thinking? And is our availability to give to and receive from others nothing other than some collective illusion? Are we deceived, trying to see God and missing the bitter reality of our daily existence? Do we see a lion in the marble and yet not see that it really blocks our way?

There *is* an answer to the boy's question and it is an answer that irritates and inspires. The answer to the boy is: "I knew there was a lion in the marble because before I saw the lion in the marble I saw it in my own heart. There is a deep secret here that I want to share with you. It was the lion in my own heart who recognized the lion in the marble."

The practice of contemplative prayer is the discipline by which we begin to "see" the living God dwelling in our own hearts. Careful attentiveness to One who makes a home in the privileged center of our being gradually leads to recognition. As we come to know and love the Father of our hearts we give ourselves over to this incredible Presence who takes possession of all our senses. By the discipline of prayer we are awakened and opened to God within who enters into our heartbeat and our breathing, into our thoughts and emotions, our hearing, seeing, touching, and tasting. It is by being awake to this God within that we also find the Presence in the world around us. Here we are again in front of the secret. It is not that we see God in the world, but that God within us recognizes God in the world. God speaks to God, Spirit speaks to Spirit, heart speaks to heart.

Contemplation, therefore, is a participating in the divine self-recognition. The divine Spirit alive in us makes our world transparent for us and opens our eyes to the presence of the divine Spirit in all that surrounds us. It is with our heart of hearts that we see the heart of our world and this explains the intimate relationship between contemplation and ministry.

Saint Francis spoke with the sun, the moon, and the animals not because he was a naïve romantic, but because his ascetic discipline awakened him to the God of his heart and enabled him to see the Lord in all that surrounded him. The Little Brothers and Sisters of Jesus deliberately choose inconspicuous and often monotonous work not because they do not see other, better possibilities, but because they recognize and want to make visible to the poorest the God whose loving care they saw in their hour of adoration. They desire to carry God in the very midst of the human struggle. The Missionaries of Charity in Calcutta experience God's presence amidst the poorest of the poor because they already experienced this presence in the intimacy of their contemplation. So, all real ministry finds its source in a well-trained heart where God dwells and is known and loved.

Knowing God in the world means knowing God "by heart" and to know God by heart is at the foundation of contemplative discipline. Finding the time and being faithful to the time with God is a very hard discipline, especially for those of us who work more often with our minds. But let us be serious about our yearning to care and make the world a better place, and let us be willing to engage in the tough and often agonizing struggle to break through all our mental defenses and know our God by heart.

Simple and obedient

We must not underestimate the intensity of this struggle. As people involved in the day-to-day we are surrounded by papers and people, by TV and cocktail parties, by demanding children and the loss of friends. We are constantly in danger of letting God's Word become tangled in the network of our responsibilities and needs, of our elaborate arguments and of the sheer verbosity all around. As those who are serious about bringing God's Word to others, we urgently need a discipline of contemplative prayer.

There are two main characteristics of contemplative prayer that seem to be particularly important: simplicity and obedience. In our contemplation let us become first and foremost simple, very simple. In prayer the Word of God descends from our mind into our heart and there becomes fruitful. Let us try diligently, then, to avoid all long inner reasoning and inner speeches, and let us focus quietly on a word or sentence. We must ruminate on it, murmur it, chew it, eat it, so that in our innermost self we can really sense its power.

Secondly, in our prayer let us become obedient. The word *obedience* comes from the word *audire*, which means to listen. Contemplative prayer calls us to listen with our hearts for the voice of Love. Let Love speak when and where it chooses and do not try to manipulate it. Let Love guide us and let us give up the control.

We are frightened of giving over the control because it may mean that God will say what we aren't expecting or what we might not want to hear. But if we listen long and deeply, God is revealed to us as a soft breeze or a still, small voice; God desires communion and comes to us in gentle compassion. Without our obedience, this listening to the God of our hearts, we remain deaf and our life grows more and more absurd. The word *absurd* includes the term *surdus*, which means deaf. The absurd life is the opposite of the obedient life.

Thus simple and obedient we come to know God by heart in our time of prayer. When we know Love in our hearts, we also recognize Love in our world, in nature, in history, and best of all in people.

This discipline of daily, faithful, communion with the Beloved is the foundation of the spiritual life underneath all we do, say, and create.

CONCLUSION

In these reflections I have tried to give a contemporary meaning to the *theoria physike*, about a vision of the nature of things, and the *praktike*, the practice and discipline of prayer. I have called the *theoria physike* the contemplative life and the *praktike* contemplative prayer. According to Evagrius, *praktike* and *theoria physike* find their culmination in *theologia*. This *theologia* is the direct knowledge of God that automatically leads to the contemplation of Divine Source of all life. Here we go beyond the practice of contemplative prayer, and even beyond the vision of the nature of things, and enter into a most intimate communion with God who calls us beloved daughters and sons. This communion of mind and heart corresponds to our deepest yearnings and is the greatest and most wonderful gift of all. It is the grace of complete unity, rest, and peace. It is the peak of our whole spiritual journey, because we somehow transcend the mundane to know and experience ourselves in the heart of God's inner life, and our world as the precious work of God's hand. In this experience we are not worrying about the quality of our prayer or the depth of our caring. The distinctions are no longer important to us. We are coming through the passage from opaqueness to transparency and there are no more blindfolds to keep us from seeing and living in the very Presence of Love.

This *theologia* in our lives is like the Mount Tabor experience in Jesus' life. In its totality it is an experience that is given rarely and only to a few. In a moment they experience the deepest and most profound intimacy, and then even they must return to the valley, having been told not to tell others what they have seen. You and I may spend the greater part of our lives not on the mountaintop but in the valley where we have the privileged call to bring Good News to the poor, but we *will* encounter God because God is Presence, Love, and Compassion.

I began with the story of the boy and the sculptor, which was meant as a parable. I thought it might help us to see the intimate relationship between our inner lives of intimacy with our first Love and our external lives of "laying down our lives" for others. I conclude with the hope that we courageously choose the life that removes the blindfolds and reveals our true identity as beloved sons and daughters of a loving Father/Mother God. And I pray that we will become God's presence to one another in this valley of tears, knowing the truth and the joy of our response to the question "Please tell me, how did you know there was a lion in the marble?"

POSTSCRIPT

White on our faces

The four chapters of this book were written as a response to some very concrete questions of English-speaking men and women religious living in Rome. When, however, I look back on these reflections and see them as a whole, it seems to me that their value might go beyond those who raised the questions. I wonder if every human being has not known in some way and at some time the desire for solitude, or inner vacancy, for prayer, and for contemplation.

Don't all men and women experience the urge to be alone with God, to create space for the encounter with Love in their deepest center, and to see more clearly and hear more deeply the truth about life and love? Mostly these desires and aspirations remain hidden or are quickly washed away by the waves of our engagements and involvements, but they never seem to vanish completely. Especially with the "big bang" of communications during the last decades, we have become so much more aware of our inner landscape. Many of us are searching for guidance to bring our inner lives more into the foreground of our consciousness with a view to greater coherency between the two. While solitude, celibacy, prayer, and contemplation are values for all people, some feel a unique desire and call to give special visibility to the inner journey by a consecrated life in which these values support us and nurture us. But whenever these values are lived out authentically and generously, what becomes visible is not a spiritual virtuosity that is good for a select few, but a way of life that speaks to many others.

Between frightening acts of the heroes of this world, there is a constant need for clowns, people who by their empty, solitary lives of inner communion with the God who dwells within speak to our "other side," offering consolation, comfort, hope, and a smile. Rome is a good city in which to become aware of the need for clowns. This large, busy, entertaining, and distracting city keeps calling us to join the lion tamers and trapeze artists who get most of the attention. But whenever the clowns appear we are reminded that what really counts is something other than the spectacular and the sensational. Clowns remind us of what happens between the scenes. The clowns show us by their "useless" behavior not simply that many of our preoccupations, worries, tensions, and anxieties need a smile, but that we too have white on our faces and that we too are called to clown a little.

I have discovered some very beautiful clowns in Rome, holy men and women whose tears always hide a smile and whose smiles always hide a tear. They have encouraged me not to wipe off the white on my face but to add some to it. I hope that you who have read this book will also feel encouraged to use more clown white and experience in your own lives the preciousness of solitude, celibacy, prayer, and contemplation.